THE POWER OF THE CITY
THE CITY OF POWER

THE POWER OF THE CITY

Whitney Museum of American Art

/ THE CITY OF POWER

CONTENTS

ACKNOWLEDGMENTS

WE WOULD LIKE to express our gratitude to Sarah Bayliss, Benjamin H.D. Buchloh, Ron Clark, Mary Kelly, and the Helena Rubinstein Fellows of the Independent Study Program for their insightful guidance as well as their welcome and invaluable assistance at every stage of this project. We also received encouragement throughout from Richard Armstrong, Richard Marshall, Lisa Phillips, David A. Ross, and Elisabeth Sussman at the Whitney Museum of American Art; Thelma Golden at the Whitney Museum at Philip Morris; Gioia Whittemore Frelinghuysen, Samantha Tsao, and Amy Mizrahi Zorn at the Whitney Museum, Downtown at Federal Reserve Plaza.

We are also grateful to the following people for their essential contributions and cooperation: Sharon Avery, Chris Dercon, Philip Glass, Jan Greben and Aldo Rossi's Studio di Architettura, Jon Hendricks, Frederick Henry and The Bohen Foundation, Jean-Noël Herlin, Stokes Howell, Hiroko Kawahara, Billy Klüver, David Stark and the Keith Haring Estate, as well as the staffs at Exit Art, Feature, Michael Klein Gallery, P.P.O.W, the United States Playing Card Company, John Weber Gallery, Jack Tilton Gallery, and The Andy Warhol Foundation for the Visual Arts, Inc.

Special thanks go to designer Alexander Ku, artists Vito Acconci, Dennis Adams, Sophie Calle, Hans Haacke, Douglas Huebler, On Kawara, Lois Nesbitt, REPOhistory, Francesc Torres, Alain Paiement, Benjamin Patterson, Dan Wiley, Krzysztof Wodiczko, and David Wojnarowicz for their generous help.

PREFACE

THIS EXHIBITION IS AN inquiry into contemporary representations and use of urban space. Unlike earlier, modernist projects of visualization of the city, the postmodernist urban vision is marked by an increasing conceptualization of space. Rather than offer mimetic descriptions of the cityscape, which imply a mastering gaze, the artists in The Power of the City / The City of Power resort to "cognitive mapping," locating their representations within everyday life, mapping the urban *topos* through strategies of urban drifting, and regarding the city as an arena for site-specific art practices.

There are two aspects to this examination, which the exhibition articulates around the axis of power. The Power of the City focuses on the concept of *dérive*, the act of aleatory drifting within or between cities and the mapping of these itineraries. Advanced in the late 1950s by the Situationist International, *dérive* constitutes an interesting aspect of Fluxus and Conceptual Art of the 1960s and 1970s. Within this exhibition, *dérive* is represented in the works of Stanley Brouwn, Daniel Buren, André Cadere, Öyvind Fahlström, Théodore Fraenkel, Douglas Huebler, On Kawara, George Maciunas, Yoko Ono, and Benjamin Patterson.

The Power of the City also examines how urban space conditions our mental space and in turn becomes the object of the constant projections of our desires, fantasies, and systems of codification. The works of Vito Acconci, Michael Banicki, Sophie Calle, Matt Mullican, Claes Oldenburg, Alain Paiement, Edward Ruscha, and David Wojnarowicz exemplify this focus.

The City of Power investigates the structures and networks of power which are laid bare within the postmodern/postindustrial urban site. The conditions of urban late capitalism, wherein dominant ideologies are everywhere both reinforced and resisted, have intensified sociopolitical and economic conflicts. Issues such as homelessness, economic strife, drugs, and political struggles, as they relate to city space, are addressed in the work of Tony Cokes, Hans Haacke, David Hammons, Jenny Holzer, Candy Jernigan, Lois Nesbitt, Aldo Rossi, Gary Simmons, Francesc Torres, Andy Warhol, and Dan Wiley.

Currently, artists are using the urban space as a site for representation. This is evident in the works of Dennis Adams, Jean-Michel Basquiat, Ilona Granet, Keith Haring, Jenny Holzer, Barbara Kruger, REPOhistory, Krzysztof Wodiczko, and the graffiti movement. This art insists that sociopolitical conflicts are intensified within city space, and that power issues can and must be addressed on site, within the urban zone. The utilization of urban space borrows from the tradition of Conceptual artists who removed art from the context of the art institution. Vito Acconci, Stanley Brouwn, Tehching Hsieh, Douglas Huebler, On Kawara, George Maciunas, Yoko Ono, Benjamin Patterson, and Adrian Piper, among others, have consistently worked outside the boundaries of formally ordered objects and also outside the art historical canon.

The three essays in this catalogue explore contemporary art practices that address city space in distinct but correlative ways. "Conceptual Art: A Spatial Perspective" offers an overview of Conceptual Art and its manifestations in urban arenas, highlighting the experience of urban space and its impact on art making. "Wandering in the City" traces historical and current concepts of cognitive mapping from Dada to the present. It reveals how artists' engagements with urban topography as the locus of everyday life have led to new paradigms of representation. "The Urban Event: Spectacle, Resistance, and Hegemony" locates the oppression and resistance within the phenomenon of the contemporary urban site. This essay foregrounds the sociopolitical and economic fragmentations which are evident within the experience of the city space and which are specifically addressed within contemporary artistic representations.

Christel Hollevoet
Karen Jones

CONCEPTUAL ART: A SPATIAL PERSPECTIVE

Timothy Nye

THE CONCEPT FOR THIS exhibition arose from a sense that the evolution of the postmodern city was affecting the way certain artists perceive the urban landscape. The postmodern city, as distinguished from the modern city, is characterized by the growing erosion of the urban infrastructure; the loss of physical and social equilibrium; and increasingly complex social and physical layers which are barely contained by communication, transportation, and judicial networks. This evolution implicitly demanded that artists respond to the space of the city, whether psychological, temporal, or physical, and to do so in a way that was impossible with conventional forms of representation. The artists in this exhibition do not paint the bright city lights or the lively pedestrian-filled streets. Rather, they seek to analyze and articulate the sensations of vast spaces and of oppressive power structures felt by the urban wanderer. Their works address cognitive representations of the city that are often described through live performance or direct interaction with the urban landscape and its inhabitants.

This exhibition spans the period from 1957 to 1992. Much of the work originated at a moment when art-making concerns turned from the art object to the conceptual record, or mapping. Although the Minimalists had already addressed anti-formalist issues and the abandonment of composition, the art object was still their primary concern. It was the work that came to be termed Conceptual or Performance Art (or a variety of other names such as Idea, Process, or Body Art) which challenged the "object form" that art production had previously assumed.

This period's theoretical debates focused on what has been termed the "dematerialization of the art object"—not always to be understood as a literal dematerialization. Objects, whether photos or texts, often exist for a documentary purpose, that is, to record information or ideas; they are not necessarily made with the intention of display. This type of documentation tends to come in the form of an ordinary snapshot or an artist's notebook, or even a performance, where the body displaces the object.

The move from the visual to the conceptual marked a shift in art making toward a distinct emphasis on the structures of language as the materials of art. In early Conceptual work, language criticizes the strictly formal/visual approaches to art making found in modernist painting and sculpture as well as the idea of the uniqueness and preciousness of the art object. An entire generation's criticism addressed Clement Greenberg's failure to convincingly articulate the difference between formalist criticism, with its inherent subjectivity, and an aesthetic of taste; such criticism was being presented as if there were a scientific method for evaluating art.

In 1965 Joseph Kosuth, the most vocal in his disdain for modernist, formally based criticism, began exhibiting photostats of entries from the dictionary. In his photostat *Water* (1965), he hoped to present the "idea of water" by removing the image itself and therefore the evidence of the artist's hand. Kosuth was attempting to bridge the gap between materials and ideas through a deemphasis of the vehicle itself, the art object. He became dissatisfied, however, with the viewer's reading of the photostat as part of the "art" and not just the "idea," and began presenting these projects in art journals, as rubber stamps, prints, and, finally, billboards. These new forms and venues were intended to further remove the work from the traditional environs of art. Although other artists made equally important contributions to Conceptual Art, Kosuth's discourse remains the most available because he articulated it in many publications on his work. In America, the same anti-formalist position was being explored simultaneously by several camps of artists (Sol LeWitt, Robert Barry, John Baldessari, Mel Bochner, Dan Graham, and Daniel Buren, to name a few). The early work of all these Conceptualists, whether in this country or abroad, offered a new form of representation, one freed from aesthetic concerns and focused exclusively on the presentation of the concept behind the work. The object was just a device to express the idea.

Most recent major exhibitions and critical writings have primarily explored Conceptual Art's deemphasis of the concern for the aesthetic. In opposition to these limited interpretations, "The Power of the City/The City of Power" reexamines Conceptual Art and its strategies as they are used to describe and map an experience of urban public space rather than pictorial space. These strategies at times end up articulating a space more psychological than physical, one that exposes the tensions created by various urban power networks. The representation of urban space and symbols of power have traditionally been illustrated through mimetic photography and figurative painting. Such representation, however, is exclusively narrative. The artists in this exhibition attempt to transcend the limitations of narrative depiction by purifying or clearing the passage from the vehicle used to convey the idea to the idea itself.

With this strategy in mind, the exhibition addresses two closely related issues. The first is how the experience of city space can be non-mimetically represented; this is the section of the exhibition dealing with the Power of the City. The second issue is how the often inequitable effects of power structures are experienced by the inhabitants of the city, and how this more psychologically oriented space can be artistically rendered; this is examined in the City of Power section of the exhibition.

Beginning in the early 1960s, a variety of artists began focusing on these questions. Stanley Brouwn posed as a disoriented pedestrian to explore the way an anonymous urbanite perceives the city and how this perception can be conveyed without standard systematic representation. *This Way Brouwn* (1961) consists of scrawled maps drawn by random pedestrians when Brouwn asked them to direct him to various locations. (He did not reveal the purpose of his requests.) His project forces one to abandon language as a vehicle of communication for a more primitive visual form. The economy of means used in the rendering of the maps encodes the participant's perceptions of urban geography. At the same time, the apparent haste and almost indecipherable nature of the maps traces the city dweller's psychological condition of impatience.

Douglas Huebler's *Duration Pieces* examine an essential issue also revealed in Brouwn's work: the close association between temporal duration and spatial expansion. Whereas time in Brouwn's work is defined by the length of the line indicating distance and, by extension, travel time, Huebler in the *Duration Pieces* describes time and space simultaneously. In 1970 he systematically gridded a small section of the city of Amsterdam. He began by selecting a random point in the city and taking what he calls an "infinite photograph" of it (a photograph focused on the farthest point in view). He then walked in that direction for thirty minutes, turned 90 degrees and took another photograph, walked in the new direction for fifteen minutes, turned 90 degrees, took another photograph, walked for seven-and-a-half minutes...and so on, until time could no longer be divided. Through the use of the "infinite photograph," Huebler implies the complete mapping of a small quadrant of Amsterdam. In Huebler's *Duration Pieces*, the element of time (the duration of time specified to walk in a certain direction) and space (the actual area covered by foot and documentation) become almost synchronous through action and documentation.

On Kawara's illusive sense of personal contact with his subject becomes a device for mapping space and time. For his *I Got Up* series, he mailed out postcards to friends, each stamped with the precise time he awakened, one a day for as long as twenty-seven consecutive days. The time, date, his present location, the addressee, and a stock postcard image of the place he was visiting provided the only information. Traditional associations of the postcard as a sentimental gesture are contradicted both by the form (stamped print) and minimal content. The tendency to depersonalize content in postcards because the message is exposed—further emphasized through Kawara's incorporation of the stamp—directs the recipient's attention to the card's passage through space and time.

Vito Acconci's performance work of the late 1960s and early 1970s examines either the self in public space or his body as public landscape. In *Following Piece* (1969), Acconci randomly follows and photographs pedestrians until they enter a private space (legally defined as one's home or a space where it would be unlawful to enter without the permission of the owner). The project addresses the conflict between public and private space and their respective claimants. Acconci distinguishes this space in a legal sense: he does not follow the pedestrian beyond the door because you cannot enter another person's home. You do have the right, however, to invade

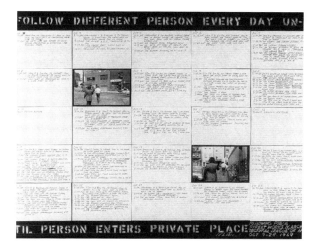

Vito Acconci, *Following Piece*, 1969

Sophie Calle, *The Shadow,* 1985

15

another individual's privacy as long as you remain in public territory. Acconci's action invades territory that otherwise might be left private, thus subverting the seeming security of neutral space by limiting his subject's enjoyment of privacy to designated spaces.

A different definition of private space is at the heart of Sophie Calle's *The Shadow* (1985). Calle asked her mother to hire a detective to follow her around. The detective is unaware of the collusion. Calle leads the detective through her daily routines and meetings. There is a perverse satisfaction in the sharing of her personal, intimate space. The detective, carrying out his duty, documents the project with photographs and written reports. This documentation becomes a map of Calle's footsteps, a permanent trace of her fleeting presence. Calle inverts the implied power structure of the enlightened detective and the unknowing victimized subject. The detective's invasion of Calle's private affairs is in fact an unspoken invitation to share the intimacies of her daily life. Like Brouwn and Acconci, Calle enlists the participants without their consent, redefining participatory modes in specific terms of social interaction.

Issues of repossession of the city are examined in Lois Nesbitt's *Gallery Labels* of 1992. On the facades of defunct galleries, Nesbitt discreetly places a label identical to those found in museums and galleries to describe works of art. The label provides the "date of extinction," accompanied by the date and reason for the closing. A map documenting the location of these extinct spaces becomes an evidentiary walking tour of the depressed art world economy. Nesbitt's transformation of these dead spaces into sculptural structures—the space itself is a ready-made sculpture—represents a kind of cultural reincarnation.

The *Rating* projects of Michael Banicki deliberately present subjective decision-making processes as objective and mathematically determined. Banicki has rated, among other things, telephone exchanges, bottle caps, black baseball teams, and storefronts. The list of items to be compared is presented on a huge grid with horizontal and vertical axes. Each item is individually compared to the other items and a preference indicated by a color-coded dot. The selection of subjects rated seems purposely arbitrary, opening Banicki's work to more metaphorical interpretations. Although his analysis of information pretends to be based on objective considerations, it is in fact a falsified objectivity, reminiscent, for instance, of the urban power network's arbitrary decisions manifested within city space. In the context of this exhibition, the grid form becomes a map of the injustices passed off as the products of intelligent and equitable decisions.

Dennis Adams confronts social injustice overtly through the construction of public structures such as bus shelters and pissoirs that contain metaphoric historical imagery. His works are best described as interventionalist sculpture masked as urban furniture. Adams inserts images of controversial historical memories into public spaces to subtly criticize the inadequacies of public assistance programs. He addresses urban power structures by jarring the viewer into thinking about the real function and implication of these structures. *Bus Shelter II* (1984-86), erected near Union Square, seems to be an ordinary bus shelter. Replacing the advertisements, however, are photographs taken at the espionage trial of Julius and Ethel Rosenberg in 1951. The Rosenbergs were tried and executed for allegedly passing military secrets to the Soviet Union. The case became notorious for the highly questionable evidence used to convict them. To affirm the connection of the case to public life, Adams situated the shelter in the vicinity of the Rosenberg's apartment. The seemingly innocuous utilitarian donation becomes a statement of the brutal injustices of governmental and judicial power, and, more specifically, an aggressive metaphor for the city's inability to really "shelter" its inhabitants. Adams' piece occupies the hidden spaces of memory as well as city life.

Candy Jernigan's *Found Dope* and *Found Dope II*, both of 1986, also attempt to probe hidden spaces. *Found Dope* collages the discoveries of Jernigan's casual strolls through her East Village neighborhood. The detritus of the drug culture that she easily finds is evidence of the rampant use of drugs in the city. *Found Dope II* is a collage of crack vials also found within a ten-block radius of her home. Each vial contains a number underneath, and the location where it was found is indicated on a map of the small quadrant of the city surrounding her apartment. The discovery of the vials in Jernigan's own neighborhood becomes a metaphor for the proximity of this problem to (our) home. The ease with which Jernigan collects the

Dennis Adams, *Bus Shelter II*, 1984–86

David Hammons, *Bliz-aard Ball Sale*, 1983

materials for her project is an indication of the overwhelming magnitude of the problem of drug abuse.

David Hammons is concerned with the difficulties of survival in the city. The photographic documentation of *Bliz-aard Ball Sale* (1983) examines the desperate measures the unemployed must take. Alluding to car window washers at traffic intersections, three-card monte scams on lower Broadway, and the other urban con games, Hammons depicts himself selling snowballs in Cooper Square. Ironically, there is a certain honesty in his con. He makes no effort to conceal the worthlessness of his wares nor is there any bullying insistence on payment for unrequested services rendered. Privileged urbanites are almost relieved that they can channel feelings of guilt into hostility, rather than be forced to confront the ugly spaces of city life.

Krzysztof Wodiczko in his *Homeless Vehicle Project* (1989) constructs a series of wheeled vehicles in which the homeless can store their possessions. The project brings attention to the issue of homelessness by engaging the natural curiosity of middle-class consumers:

> The middle classes are well trained as consumers. As good consumers, they know how to...accurately evaluate the "value" of new functional and symbolic form that appears before their commodity-tuned eyes. Every time we see a tool, we look at its shape, its details, its movements, and its position in a particular environment. We guess what it does, who would use it, and what situation creates the need for it. How important is [it] to have? If we have not seen such a tool before, we are curiously surprised by its appearance. We examine each movement of its operator in relation to the movement of the tool. We notice how the tool transforms its environment and wonder what this means to the user and to us. [1]

Wodiczko is trying to reawaken the sensitivity we have lost through overexposure. His strategy of arousing curiosity rather than guilt creates a positive forum for confrontation with an urban reality that often is shamefully avoided.

Jenny Holzer also acts as an urban interventionist. One of her electronic billboards installed on Times Square displays the words "Protect me from what I want." The pedestrian's expectation of a solicitous message or product promotion is confounded by a concise political commentary that alerts consumers to the seductive powers of consumer-oriented messages. Holzer understands that advertising does not fulfill but creates needs. Day-to-day survival is made even more difficult if one is impelled to extravagant desires. Holzer's form of social advertising attempts to awaken us to the problem and fence off those tempting, improvident spaces occupied by boutiques and department stores.

Hans Haacke's real estate pieces expose the unethical composition of corporate America. Yet what he uncovers, though unethical, is not unlawful. His *Shapolsky et al. Manhattan Real Estate Holdings, a Real-Time Social System, as of May 1, 1971* displays the vast slum holdings of the Shapolsky Real Estate Corporation. The piece consists of 142 photos of the tenement facades and vacant lots, documents, and a map indicating the location of the properties in Harlem and the Lower East Side. The vast detail and size of the piece visually reinforces the depth of Shapolsky's contribution to the housing crisis in New York. The photographic documentation, even in its neutral presentation, clearly shows the shameful condition of the buildings, demonstrating the depth of Shapolsky's negligence and unscrupulousness. Haacke constructs his narrative by using only publicly available material. His criticism, therefore, is not only directed at overturning the immaculate corporate image, exposing the corruption behind these padlocked doors and barred windows, but it is also designed to show that part of the problem rests in the public's apathy.

There is another context in which Haacke's *Shapolsky* piece can be viewed. Discussing the work, Rosalyn Deutsche noted that for Haacke "a work's meaning is always incomplete, changing 'as of' different temporal situations; that the work incorporates the responses it evokes and mutates accordingly to the uses to which it is put...."[2] The idea that a Haacke work can reflect "different temporal situations" is ironically relevant to the present context—that of the last exhibition to be held in this space.

Francesc Torres distances himself from the specific daily traumas of urban existence, commenting instead on a more general urban phe-

21

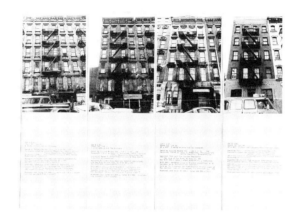

Hans Haacke, *Shapolsky et al. Manhattan Real Estate Holdings, a Real-Time Social System, as of May 1, 1971*, 1971

Francesc Torres, *Assyrian Paradigm*, 1980

nomenon: "what the people in power fear the most: the chance factor in life and historical processes."[3] His *Assyrian Paradigm*, originally made in 1980 and reconfigured for this exhibition, is a model of a generic city composed almost entirely of playing cards. The title suggests the rapid rise, precarious tenure, and consequent fall of the Assyrian Empire, but in contemporary terms it concerns issues of mutable civic structures and mortality. The card houses, although held together with adhesive, are still extremely fragile. A viewer passing by could easily topple one with the tail of a coat. In fact, Torres fully intends that certain sections of his city collapse. The obelisk at the center contains a clear box housing two dice. The box periodically shakes them, implying that a city's destiny is as unpredictable as a roll of the dice. In the end, civic laws and safeguards can only do so much to circumvent disaster.

Through cognitive mapping, intervention with political power networks, and interaction with urban inhabitants, the artists in this exhibition attempt to eliminate barriers between their conceptions of urban space, the power that the city exerts on its inhabitants, and the materials used to realize these impressions. This has led several of the Conceptual artists in the exhibition to consider the psychological dimensions of city space. The exhibition thus explores the interplay between internal and external spaces, exposing tensions and recording urban pathologies. It suggests that urban planners and architects have a moral obligation to consider our environment in the psychological terms revealed by the artists' diagnoses of our urban condition.

Notes

1. Quoted in *Art Random*, (Kyoto: Kyoto Shoin International Co., 1991), p.2.

2. Rosalyn Deutsche, "Property Values: Hans Haacke, Real Estate and the Museum," in *Hans Haacke: Unfinished Business*, exhibition catalogue (New York: The New Museum of Contemporary Art, 1986), p.23.

3. Artist's statement in *Francesc Torres: Field of Action*, exhibition catalogue (Ithaca, New York: Herbert F. Johnson Museum of Art, Cornell Universtiy, 1982), p.32.

WANDERING IN THE CITY
FLÂNERIE TO *DÉRIVE* AND AFTER: THE COGNITIVE MAPPING OF URBAN SPACE

Christel Hollevoet

THE POWER OF THE CITY

URBAN ROAMING HAS BEEN a recurrent and deliberate attitude among literary and artistic bohemians from Romanticism, via Dada and Surrealism, to the Situationist International and Fluxus, Conceptual Art, and contemporary art practices. The phenomenon of urban drifting, successively coined *flânerie* and *dérive*, is a form of spatial and conceptual investigation of the metropolis pervasive throughout modernism and extending into postmodernism.

The French poet Charles Baudelaire, in his review of the Salon of 1846, exalted the aesthetic of urban transitoriness by describing the ephemeral beauty of the marginal: "the thousands of floating existences—criminals and kept women—which drift about in the underworld of a great city," which fascinated the roaming *flâneur*.[1] Baudelaire exalted the urban dweller's feeling of the sublime in the midst of modern Paris, "enveloped and steeped as though in an atmosphere of the marvellous."[2] Almost twenty years later, in "The Painter of Modern Life"(1863), he specified: "By 'modernity' I mean the ephemeral, the fugitive, the contingent, the half of art whose other half is the eternal and the immutable."[3]

Baudelaire's *flâneur* is the point of departure for a long series of artists who tackled the problem of apprehending and representing the situations and atmospheres encountered in the public spaces of the modern city. In the early twentieth century, the fascination for simultaneity in the cityscape and the mythology of modernity were exalted primarily by the Futurists, but the Dadaists in their own way incorporated bits and pieces of urban life through the techniques of collage and assemblage. They were also responsible for one of the first instances of performance in urban space.

Théodore Fraenkel,
*Excursions DADA: Saint Julien
le Pauvre,* 1921

Théodore Fraenkel,
*Excursions & Visites DADA: 1ère Visite:
Église Saint Julien le Pauvre,* 1921

At the time of their association with Dada, Louis Aragon, André Breton, Paul Éluard, Théodore Fraenkel, Francis Picabia, Georges Ribemont-Dessaignes, Tristan Tzara, and others took Baudelaire's words literally: "Is there anything more charming, more fertile and positively exciting than the commonplace?"[4] They organized a series of excursions to intentionally meaningless, common places, such as the *1ère Visite*, on Thursday, April 14, 1921, at 3pm, to the church of Saint Julien le Pauvre, where Breton read a manifesto. Other visits were planned to the Louvre, Buttes Chaumont, Gare Saint-Lazare, Mont du Petit Cadenas, and Canal de l'Ourcq, but ultimately never took place.[5] The announcement specifies that the visits were to places which "have really no reason for being," that one should not look for the picturesque, historical relevance, or sentimental value. It even alludes to possible destruction. Typical of Dadaist anti-art practices, these excursions were tributes to life and to the banal; they were intended to mystify the "bourgeois" by attacking their monuments, while celebrating the possibility of discovering, even in the most banal places, some mystery elicited by one person's encounter with a specific place.

In May 1924, Breton and Aragon, along with Morise and Vitrac, set out on an aleatory walking trip to physically experience drifting in real space. Their itinerary between cities drawn by lot led them from Blois to Romorantin.[6] It was after this trip that Breton wrote the preface to *Poisson soluble*, which became the manifesto of Surrealism.[7]

The Surrealist exaltation of chance encounters, the unconscious, irrational drives and attractions, perplexing situations, and elusive atmospheres finds a specific expression in the stochastic experience of city life, for instance, in André Breton's *Nadja* (1928) or *L'amour fou* (1937). Louis Aragon typically begins *Le paysan de Paris* (1926) with "Le passage de l'Opéra," which immediately evokes Baudelaire's exaltation of the ephemeral beauty of the city's atmospheres:

> Metaphysic of places, you are the hand that rocks children and winds their dreams. Our entire mental substance washes onto these shores of gooseflesh and the unknown. I cannot step into the past without encountering this sensation of the uncanny which beset me when I was still amazement personified and; in a specific setting, recognized some unexplained coherence, seconded by my heart.[8]

Aragon further describes the arcades *(passages)* as obsolete icons of the modernist myth and as sanctuaries of the transitory, a concept that became Walter Benjamin's greatest fascination.

In his unfinished project *Das Passagen-Werk* (1927-40), Benjamin in turn elaborated on Baudelaire's and Aragon's idea of the *flâneur* indulging in aimless strolls in the Parisian arcades and later amidst the crowds on Baron Haussmann's new boulevards. His projected book, dedicated to "Paris, capital of the nineteenth century," included a chapter devoted to the *flâneur*, or rather to the city which was the terrain of the *flâneur*. Echoing Aragon's words, Benjamin likened the *flâneur's* experience of the city to that of a child who perceives it as a collection of places and situations charged with mythical power.

Aragon's text is of seminal importance in Benjamin's 1928 essay, "Surrealism: The Last Snapshot of the European Intelligentsia."[9] Benjamin faults Surrealism's representation of mythology and oneirism for their own sakes, while celebrating the revolutionary powers of obsoleteness. The enigmas of the present, he explains, can be resolved through the obsolete past, in a dialectical process similar to that of dream mechanisms. According to the Benjaminian dialectical method of history, one awakens to the present by means of reliving the past as if it were a dream—and this past is embodied in places.[10] At the time he was writing the Surrealism essay, Benjamin was already developing the *Passagen-Werk,* inspired by the arcades of Paris, in which he replaced the historical approach of the past by archaeology, or topography, substituting the criteria of space for that of time. His inquiry into the past is indeed an anachronistic recollection of places and situations, rather than a linear tracing of moments or events.[11] This urban drifting impulse and the mapping of the geographical *topos*, or place, are extremely significant for later artistic practices. They signal a pervasive view of urban geography as locus of the experience of modern life and announce the necessity for new paradigms of artistic representation.

One of the leitmotifs of the *Passagen-Werk* is a vision of the city as an interior, or apartment, where the neighborhoods are like different rooms, and the advertising signs are like pictures on the walls of a living room.

Benjamin contrasted the crowds, the collective, the proletariat of the streets to the bourgeois, imbued with false subjectivity and individualism, in his private apartment. The city was the "interior" of the collective, its home.[12]

The *flâneur*, the distanced observer of modernity who haunted the city, first strolled through the arcades, then amidst street crowds, and eventually through department stores, where he became a consumer, where his experience embodied commodity fetishism, the seeking of "nouveautés" and "spécialités."[13]

The *flâneur's* investigation of the city is an early attempt to read the essence of modernity in urban spatial configuration.[14] The topography of modernity was a concern for many artists who depicted the dynamics of the city in two-dimensional representations. However, as opposed to paintings, whose vertical planes evoke the window of the perceptive model, representations of urban space very early on resorted to the horizonality of the map.[15]

Cubist-influenced works such as Mondrian's abstract grid compositions—*Broadway Boogie Woogie*, for instance—combine a grid/map system of representation which Rosalind Krauss has described as typical of modernism.[16] Yve-Alain Bois, writing on Mondrian's painting *New York City* (1942), which the artist worked on with the canvas on the floor, incorporates Leo Steinberg's concept of the "flatbed" to explain the shift from the vertical picture plane to horizontality:

> *New York City* is one of the first "flatbeds," one of the first examples of the horizontal reversal that Steinberg considered in quasi-Lévi-Straussian terms as a passage from nature to culture in Robert Rauschenberg's art: "palimpsest, canceled plate, printer's proof, trial blank, chart, map, aerial view. Any flat documentary surface that tabulates information is a relevant analogue of his picture plane—radically different from the transparent projection plane with its optical correspondence to man's visual field." Steinberg says that the "flatbed"—traverse section, symbolic—arises from action, as the verticality of the picture plane in the Renaissance arose from vision. There is a fundamental difference—a gulf, however small—between representing action and fulfilling it.[17]

For this reason, artists hailing from groups such as the Situationist International, Fluxus, and Conceptual Art dismissed painting in their

apprehension of urban space. Their artistic production consists of action —
in the case that interests us here, a spatial investigation of the actual city
through urban roaming.

Michel de Certeau makes this clear in his essay "Spatial Practices,"
where he outlines the difference between the scopic pulsion in traditional
pictorial representations of cities and what he calls the "blind knowledge"
one has when walking through urban space. He points out that from the
Middle Ages on, cities have been represented in totalizing panoramas seen
from an imaginary bird's-eye view, where the urban complexity is made leg-
ible and its opaqueness transformed into a transparent text. De Certeau
opposes this traditional scopophilic apprehension to that of the cityscape
grasped from below, where the legibility of the urban text(ure) is blurred
and its clarity elusive:

> The ordinary practitioners of the city live "down below," below the threshold at which vis-
> ibility begins. They walk—an elementary form of this experience of the city: they are
> walkers, *Wandersmänner*, whose bodies follow the thicks and thins of an urban "text" they
> write without being able to read it. [18]

This other field of experience, epitomized by urban roaming, was
explored by artists whose work pertains to the field of performance or happenings, rather than to the production of art objects. In these works, reality and
representation are merged; as art locates itself in real time and real space, it can
only be documented through traces, such as texts, photographs, and maps.

In the late 1950s, the artists' collaborative Internationale Situationniste
(1958-69), an offshoot of the literary group Internationale Lettriste (1952-
57), introduced into art a development of the literary concept of *flânerie*.
They called their concept *dérive*, a non-optical apprehension of urban space
anticipating what Fredric Jameson coined "cognitive mapping." Pronounc-
ing the preeminence of the topographical in postmodernity, Jameson
proposed that:

a model of political culture appropriate to our own situation will necessarily have to raise spatial issues as its fundamental organizing concern. I will therefore provisionally define...an aesthetic of *cognitive mapping*.... the alienated city is above all a space in which people are unable to map (in their minds) either their own positions or the urban totality in which they find themselves.... Disalienation in the traditional city, then, involves the practical reconquest of a sense of place and the construction or reconstruction of an articulated ensemble which can be retained in memory and which the individual subject can map and remap along the moments of mobile, alternative trajectories.[19]

Like the labyrinth wrought by the Greek mythological architect Daedalus, the city invites the *flâneur* to get lost for the sake of grasping its impenetrable maze, so close to that of our mental space. Walter Benjamin's chapter on the *flâneur* bore as epigraph the words of a madman: "I travel to know my geography."[20] This anticipates the efforts of the Lettrists and the Situationist International. The Lettrists advocated the replacement of aesthetics by ethics. Deriving their sense of urgency from Surrealism, they went beyond art, which they found elitist and too individualistic, and promoted a total revolution of everyday life through cultural experimentation. The critique and transformation of everyday life had been theorized by both André Breton and Henri Lefebvre, and the Situationists owe much to the first through the intermediary of the second, but they felt they had to revive the Surrealists' initial revolutionary urgency and their project of subversive irruption of art in everyday life, which by the 1950s had been abandoned.[21]

In 1953, the Situationist precursor Ivan Chtcheglov, in "Formulary for a New Urbanism," countered the Dadaists' praise of the banal, claiming the need to counteract the boredom experienced in cities, where the "poetry of the billboards" no longer was effective, where one should seek to discover new mysteries through systematic drifting in urban space. Chtcheglov named this drifting *dérive*. He argued for a new urbanism that would allow for play and experiments, and favor psychogeographical games, which would be an improvement over "the ridiculous labyrinth in the Jardin des Plantes, at the entry to which is written (height of absurdity, Ariadne unemployed): *Games are forbidden in the labyrinth*." [22]

The Situationists defined a specifically urban aesthetic of atmospheres

31

and situations,[23] and elaborated the concept of *dérive*, theorized by Guy Debord in 1955 as the fugitive encounter of various atmospheres while aimlessly drifting in a city. The aleatory element here is less important than the psychogeographical relief, i.e., the effect the city's various areas have on our affect,[24] best exemplified in these words:

> I can think of only one thing that can compete with the beauty of the subway maps posted in Paris, and that is the two ports at dusk painted by Claude Lorrain...depicting the very borderline of two extremely dissimilar urban ambiances. One must understand that in speaking here of beauty I don't have in mind plastic beauty—the new type of beauty can only be a beauty of situations—but simply the particularly moving presentation, in both cases, of a sum of possibilities.[25]

The Situationists combined arts and experimental techniques to construct an integral milieu, according to the theory they called "unitary urbanism." This theory designates, contrary to modernist functionalism, the active participation in and experience of the social space of cities. It posits urban space as a playground where everyone interacts, and which everyone mentally recreates and constantly transforms. One participates in creating the urban environment as one discovers and constructs it.

The gathering of urban ambiances by means of the *dérive* evokes Baudelaire's and Benjamin's *flâneur*, but is especially reminiscent of the Dadaist itineraries in the 1920s. Debord narrates a *dérive* of 1956:

> On Tuesday, 6 March 1956 10 A.M., G.E. Debord and Gil J. Wolman meet in the rue des Jardins-Paul and head north in order to explore the possibilities of traversing Paris at that latitude. Despite their intentions they quickly find themselves drifting toward the east and traverse the upper section of the 11th arrondissement, an area whose poor commercial standardization is a good example of repulsive petit-bourgeois landscape. The only pleasing encounter is the store at 160, rue Oberkampf: "Delicatessen—Provisions A. Breton"....Upon studying the terrain the Lettrists feel able to discern the existence of an important psychogeographic hub [*plaque tournante*]...opening out onto at least four significant psychogeographical bearings.... [26]

Unlike the Surrealists, the Situationists did not want to aestheticize life; they rejected the primacy of the individual, dreams, the unconscious, and the sublimation of desires and fantasies, launching the famous May '68 slogan: "Take your desires for reality." They advocated increased consciousness, direct action, and systematic intervention in actual life.[27] Debord insisted that "*dérive* and situation go beyond the 'imbecile strolls' of the Surrealists for the first, and beyond its usage in existentialist philosophy for the second."[28]

Even though the Situationists' debt to Dada and Surrealism is undeniable and the concept of psychogeography itself appears as the logical outcome of Surrealist literature, the shift from Baudelaire's and Aragon's *flânerie* to Debord's *dérive* is significant. The Situationists rejected art objects and aesthetic concerns in favor of social realities and life situations. They initiated topographical experiments connected to the revolution of everyday life and the production of psychogeographic maps that charted the sudden changes of ambiance and distinct psychic atmospheres encountered while drifting in a city, such as in Guy Debord's *The Naked City* or *Guide psychogéographique de Paris*, both of 1957.

✳

Since the 1960s, artists have shifted from the representation of urban space to a mode of presentation in which the city becomes an arena for site-specific sculptures and performances. In this process they attempt to compensate for the sense of dislocation and alienation epitomized by the practice of *dérive* by positioning themselves in the incommensurable through cognitive mapping.

In the 1960s, the international neo-Dada group Fluxus, founded by George Maciunas, announced its intention to "promote living art, anti-art, NON-ART REALITY to be grasped by all peoples." [29] On July 3, 1962, a *Fluxus Sneak Preview* was organized at the end of a daylong itinerary through Paris,

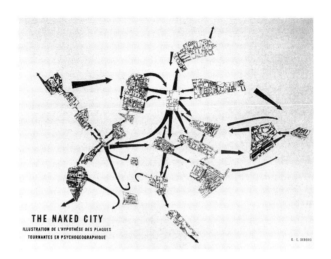

Guy Debord, *The Naked City*, 1957

Benjamin Patterson, *Invitation-map for Benjamin Patterson's Exhibit at Robert Filliou's Galerie Légitime, Followed by a Fluxus Sneak Preview*, 1962

where Benjamin Patterson and Robert Filliou interacted with the people who had come to the places on the invitation flyer at the times of day indicated. The itinerary, which constituted the exhibition of the American artist Benjamin Patterson at the Galerie Légitime, consisted of a tour of Paris from 4am to 9:30pm, from the Porte Saint-Denis to the café La Coupole, followed by the *Fluxus Sneak Preview* at the Galerie Girardon, starting at 10:40pm. Robert Filliou's Galerie Légitime, created in January 1962, was a hat (*casquette*) bought by the artist ten years before in Tokyo. The "Galerie" was later stolen in Germany, but was replaced soon after by another hat. The Galerie Légitime exhibitions took place in the public space of the street, "under the hat." The idea had come to Filliou as he observed street sellers in the Paris quarter Le Marais, where he lived at the time, who were illegally selling "genuine cheap Swiss watches" hidden under their coats. Filliou liked the idea of a similarly subversive and itinerant art gallery. He maintained that art had to come down from the "high spheres" into the streets—literally. There are no art objects to see or buy in his gallery/hat— only people to meet. The person in the hat, Filliou, accompanied Patterson, the performing artist, as the gallerist.[30]

This Fluxus itinerary, mapped on the invitation designed by Patterson, is formally reminiscent of Debord's *Naked City* and *Guide psychogéographique de Paris* and stems from a similar practice of *dérive*; it is also close in spirit to the Dada excursions. Fluxus happenings share Debord's critique of the spectator's passivity, as articulated in his book *Society of the Spectacle* (1967). They reflect the Situationist exaltation of systematic intervention, deliberately experimental behavior, and playful, nonsensical gestures, inspired by Johan Huizinga's *Homo Ludens: A Study of the Play Element in Culture*. Thus the "Psychogeographical Game of the Week" published in the Lettrist journal *Potlatch* (no.1):

> In accordance with what you are seeking, choose a country, a more or less populated city, a more or less busy street. Build a house. Furnish it. Use decorations and surroundings to the best advantage. Choose the season and the time of day. Bring together the most suitable people, with appropriate records and drinks. The lighting and the conversation should obviously be suited to the occasion, as should be the weather or your memories. If there has been no error in your calculations, the result should satisfy you. [31]

This advocacy of games and everyday life experience (against Surrealism's alleged reactionary escape from reality) is echoed in the playful practices of Fluxus artists. Yoko Ono, for example, wrote scores such as the *City Pieces,* proposing to "Walk all over the city with an empty baby carriage" (winter 1961), or "Step in all the puddles in the city" (fall 1963); or the *Map Pieces,* which read: "Draw a map to get lost" (spring 1964), or (summer 1962):

> Draw an imaginary map.
> Put a goal mark on the map where you
> want to go.
> Go walking on an actual street according
> to your map.
> If there is no street where it should be
> according to the map, make one by putting
> the obstacles aside.
> When you reach the goal, ask the name of
> the city and give flowers to the first
> person you meet.
> The map must be followed exactly, or the
> event has to be dropped altogether.
> Ask your friends to write maps.
> Give your friends maps. [32]

The *Free Flux-Tours* organized through New York in May 1976 evoke both the Situationist use of play in unitary urbanism and the Dadaist *1ère Visite* of April 1921. These tours are inquiries into an "unknown" city, whose mysterious maze has to be penetrated through the guidance of Fluxus gurus. But they also point to the crucial concern in artistic practices from the late 1950s to the 1970s for the topographical apprehension of urban space, or mapping of places and itineraries. They signal a shift from the avant-garde critique of art to the critique of everyday life; from avant-garde opposition to the popular from "outside and above" to participation in it from the inside.

FREE FLUX-TOURS

(EXCEPT FOR COST OF TRANSPORTATION & MEALS IF ANY)

May 1: MAYDAY guided by Bob Watts, call 226-3422 for transportation arrangements.
May 3: FRANCO AMERICAN TOUR, by Alison Knowles & Robert Filliou, 2 pm at 80 Wooster st.
May 4: TOUR FOR FOREIGN VISITORS, arranged by George Brecht, start noon at 80 Wooster st.
May 5: ALLEYS, YARDS & DEAD ENDS, arranged by G. Maciunas, start 3 pm at 80 Wooster st.
May 6: ALEATORIC TOUR, arranged by Jonas Mekas, meet at noon at 80 Wooster st.
May 7: MUSIC TOUR & LECTURE, by Yoshimasa Wada, start at 2 pm at 80 Wooster st.
May 8: GALLERIES, guided by Larry Miller, start at noon at 80 Wooster st.
May 9: SUBTERRANEAN TOUR I, guided by Geoff Hendricks, start at noon at 80 Wooster st.
May 9: SUBTERRANEAN DANGER by Charles Bergengren, start 11 pm at 47 st. & Park av. island.
May 10 & 11: at 6am go to 17 Mott street and eat Wonton soup (says Nam June Paik).
May 12: SUBTERRANEAN TOUR III, arranged by George Maciunas, start 7 pm at 80 Wooster st.
May 13: SOUVENIR HUNT, meet at noon at 80 Wooster st.
May 14: SOHO CURB SITES, guided by Peter Van Riper, meet at 3:30pm at 80 Wooster st.
May 15: EXOTIC SITES, guided by Joan Mathews, meet 3 pm at Oviedo Restaurant, 202 W 14 st.
May 16: ALL THE WAY AROUND & BACK AGAIN, by Peter Frank, meet at noon 80 Wooster

George Maciunas, *Free Flux-Tours*, May 1976

There were similar enterprises among Conceptual artists. In 1962, Stanley Brouwn asked people in the streets of Amsterdam to direct him to randomly chosen locations. He gave them a note pad, on which some drew their proposed itinerary. The pages were then stamped "this way brouwn" by the artist. On the one hand, *This Way Brouwn* epitomizes the city as a maze, eliciting a sense of dislocation and alienation, and the concomitant necessity for cognitive mapping, for an intelligible location of the self in the incommensurable.[33] On the other hand, as in the collaborative Fluxus tours, social interaction is pivotal, as is the annihilation of the artist/author trope: the drawings are made by the anonymous passersby and no less anonymously signed with the mechanical stroke of a rubber stamp.

In a similar vein, Douglas Huebler, in *Variable Piece #4, Paris, France* (1970) leaves it up to the piece's owner to perpetuate the mapping process *ad infinitum*. This conceptual work juxtaposes a map of Paris, on which a point has been randomly marked in ink, and a photograph taken at the actual site to which the point corresponds. The discrepancy between mapped locations and photographs of the sites is that between the index and the icon. The incongruence between the intelligible and the perceptible elicits something strange and powerful, an effect that recurs in Huebler's work.

Mapping the unmappable seems to be Huebler's aim in *Variable Piece #1, New York City* (1968), where he located the elevators of four Manhattan buildings on a map and used them to form the four corners of a square traced with adhesive tape. This constitutes the mapping of random, mobile, and vertical movement. This square is then duplicated, at double scale, mapping static and permanent locations. A third square in turn duplicates the second one in the same scale relationship. The exact places in the actual city corresponding to the four corners of the largest square on the map were marked by pieces of adhesive tape placed on four moving vehicles. These vehicles ultimately mapped horizontal and changing directions conditioned by chance.[34]

Huebler's *Variable Works (in Progress)/Düsseldorf, Germany-Turin, Italy* (1970-71), which consisted in hitchhiking from Düsseldorf to Turin, evokes the Surrealists' aleatory trip of 1924. Huebler's ultimate decision, after failing to reach Italy, to realize instead his *Alternative Piece, Paris, 1970* (1970)

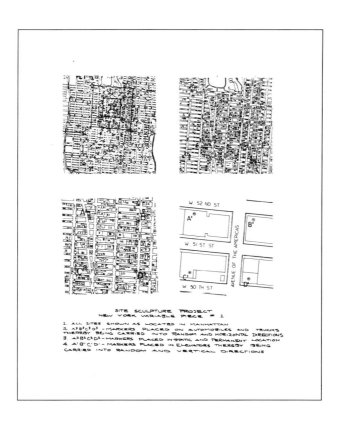

Douglas Huebler, *Variable Piece #1, New York City,* 1968

recalls Debord's essay "Theory of the Dérive," [35] which promoted purpose-less displacements. Huebler wandered in the Paris metro, flipping a coin to determine when and where to get out. He took photographs of the site as he saw it, randomly, as he ascended to the street. [36] Huebler's take on urban situations thus evokes the Dada technique of randomness, while also echo-ing Debord's view that "the element of chance is less determinant than one might think: from the *dérive* point of view, cities have a psychogeo-graphical relief, with constant currents, fixed points and vortices which strongly discourage entry into or exit from certain zones." [37] Huebler's sub-terranean itinerary and sudden emergence to the surface of the city in *Alternative Piece,* however, is randomly determined—for critical purposes: by counteracting the process of selection inherent to photography, he cri-tiques the structural impossibility of objective, comprehensive, realist representation. [38]

The unique, durable art object created by the artist has been replaced by the concept of transience, by a continual shift between reality and repre-sentation, where the art work comprises the documentation of something that occurred in a specific place, at a specific moment in time, in actual real-ity. In a supplement to Vito Acconci's periodical *0 to 9,* subtitled *Streetworks,* the statement for one of Adrian Piper's performances in the streets of Man-hattan (spring 1969) indicates the times and locations she would appear on a certain day. Similarly, André Cadere performed daily urban strolls, carry-ing incongruous striped poles. Daniel Buren, in April 1968, had two sandwichmen ambulating in front of the Musée d'Art Moderne de la Ville de Paris carrying white-and-green striped panels; at the same time, a simi-lar work of huge dimensions was pasted on the interior walls of the museum. Simultaneously, about two hundred billboards had been subversively covered with small white-and-green striped posters throughout the city. Buren's repetitive work—deprived of exchange value, extending from interior to exterior spaces, appearing on both static and mobile supports—questioned the object status of art, presenting it as the fragment of a discourse. [39]

In *Seven Ballets in Manhattan* (May 27-June 2, 1975), Buren developed the idea of mapping an itinerary—a choreography in this instance. During seven days, groups of five people carrying panels with colored stripes walked

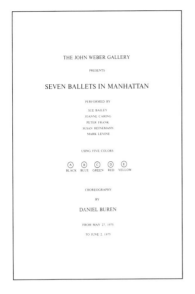

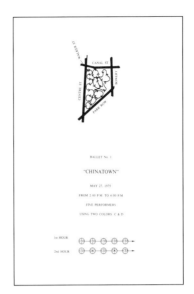

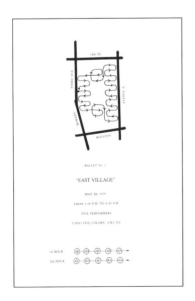

Daniel Buren, *Seven Ballets in Manhattan*, May 27– June 2, 1975

the streets of Manhattan, following choreographies devised by Buren. Each day they performed a different choreography in a new area.[40] Their aimless, purposeless, but regulated strolling intrigued passersby. The uniqueness of the performance resided in its ephemerality, and the significance of the repetitive stripes depended on their place—or itinerancy—in actual space.

Nine years earlier, in his *Bob Hope Mao Tse Tung Demonstration* of 1966, Öyvind Fahlström had performers carry placards of the American actor and the Chinese leader in the streets of New York, while the reactions of passersby were recorded on film and tape. Observers drew their own conclusions about this eruption of world-famous characters in the streets, which parodied the leveling process of media culture. The event, which was part of the series *9 Evenings: Theater and Engineering*, organized by Billy Klüver, Robert Rauschenberg, and others, was conceived as "total theater," fusing art and everyday life through the use of new technologies.

Debord's celebration of the use of maps and the practice of "possible rendez-vous" [41] is evoked in On Kawara's *I Went*, an archival record on photocopied maps of his daily itineraries in the cities he was in, as well as *I Met*, where he recorded the people he encountered. On Kawara raised spatial expansion to a global scale in the intercontinental *dérives* he engaged in from 1968 to 1979, represented in the *I Got Up* postcards sent from New York to Tokyo, Paris, Berlin, Düsseldorf, and Mexico City; and from New York to Paris, etc. This *dérive* is the end of strolling, whose walking pace is replaced by the "instantaneity of ubiquity." [42] The material boundaries and perceptive reality of cities have lost power to invisible, immaterial dimensions; the perceptible has given way to the intelligible. The slow *flâneur* who used to roam the arcades with a turtle on a leash[43] has been replaced by travelers in permanent transit; the boulevards have given way to airline networks. As Paul Virilio puts it: "In all likelihood, the essence of what we insist on calling urbanism is composed/decomposed by these transfer, transit and transmission systems, these transport and transmigration networks whose immaterial configuration reiterates the cadastral organization and the building of monuments." [44]

The French art historian Jean-Hubert Martin, who traces the *dérive* back to Dadaism and, via the Situationists, to On Kawara, Douglas Huebler, and

Daniel Buren,
Seven Ballets in Manhattan, 1975

Öyvind Fahlström, *Bob Hope
Mao Tse Tung Demonstration from
"Kisses Sweeter than Wine,"* 1966

Daniel Buren, cites other examples of artists' mapping and drifting processes. Among them are the meticulous daily itineraries traced by Didier Bay and Christian Boltanski, Paul-Armand Gette and Jean Le Gac's happening in Paris, from June 1970 to January 1971. During these seven months, they sent nine invitations for nine different journeys to locations which, like the Dada excursions, were both banal and mysterious.[45]

Unlike the reified objects produced by individual artists, Fluxus happenings and Conceptual events represent radical intrusions and interventions upon the actual physical configuration of the city. Interaction with the urban dwellers, collaborative performances, integration of art and everyday life can all be recognized as the ultimate results of Surrealist and Situationist theories. This heritage carries with it the continuous and fluctuating practice of aimless roaming through aleatory itineraries in cities, and its corollary, the loss of self to the power of the city.

Vito Acconci's *Following Piece* (1969) documents a performance where he followed people in the streets of New York to the point where they entered their apartments. This is reminiscent of Edgar Allan Poe's story "Man of the Crowd," exalted by both Baudelaire and Benjamin, where the narrator/*flâneur*/detective distinguishes someone in a crowd and follows him for a whole day.[46] The narrator of Poe's story reflects that the world cannot be known, "does not let itself be read," an inscrutability also characteristic of Sophie Calle's *The Shadow* (1985). At Calle's request, her mother hired a private detective to follow her for several days. Calle knows she is being followed and chooses a deliberate itinerary through Paris, to places that evoke private memories. The detective, who is systematically recording every move she makes, every place she goes to, ends up producing an "objective" description of her roaming which, of course, totally misses the personal connotations of the sites.

✳

The problem faced by contemporary artists tackling urban space was twofold: first, how to best apprehend the experience of urban space not as spectator but as actor; second, how to best re-present urban space, not in terms of figure and ground, on a two-dimensional plan, but in active physical and mental intervention. The first question was solved through *dérive* and its ulterior forms in Fluxus and Conceptual Art; the second by the topographical mapping of drifting processes, or cognitive mapping.[47]

If at first it was thought that the reality, the essence of the modern city could be known through penetrating visual observation and description and encapsulated in an icon, later urban situations came to be grasped in more conceptual terms. They were represented through a different register of signs: either the symbolic, with conventions based on an arbitrary relation to the referent; or the indexical, with traces based on a physical relation to the referent. The work is an index of an ephemeral situation or immaterial concept; it remains a sign and can never be posited as an art "object." It is hardly ever more than a piece of paper, a relic, archival material. It has the precariousness of an invitation or a poster, of On Kawara's *I Got Up* postcards or his *I Went* photocopied maps; or of Douglas Huebler's ephemeral adhesive tape put on moving vehicles, which extended the mapping of his *Variable Piece #1, New York City*. These forms of apprehension of urban space emphasize the artist's conception and performance of the work, at the expense of the production of a unique art "object"—object quality having been questioned since Marcel Duchamp. The art "object" becomes the city itself: Marcel Duchamp declared in 1917 that the newly built Woolworth Building was a readymade; Arman announced in October 1961 that Manhattan was a giant accumulation, which he publicly "signed" on the Lower East Side;[48] Daniel Buren in April 1968 used the walls of Paris as support for his striped paper; and the same transformation from object to urban situation determined Robert Filliou's exhibitions at the Galerie Légitime.

Collaboratives such as the Situationist International or Fluxus signaled the end of the centered subject, i.e., the creative artist, the autonomous "bourgeois ego, or monad." [49] They favored cultural practices that crossed the boundaries between disciplines, denigrated reified commodities, and rejected the mirage of self-expression for cognitive mapping. The deconstruction of the mystique of the avant-garde, the "waning of affect," and the end of idiosyncratic style that characterize postmodernity [50] contextual-

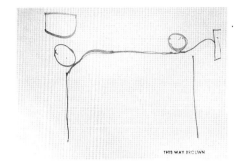

Stanley Brouwn,
*This Way Brouwn, 25-2-61,
26-2-61*, 1961

On Kawara, *I Got Up,* 1970

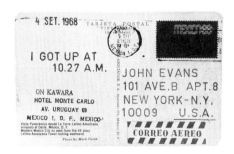

46

ize the reiteration of this cognitive mapping of the urban *topos*, apprehended through *dérive*. As Jameson put it, cognitive mapping is called upon to "enable a situational representation on the part of the individual subject to that vaster and properly unrepresentable totality which is the ensemble of society's structure as a whole." [51]

Jameson ultimately tried to "rethink these specialized geographical and cartographic issues in the terms of social space." [52] The concept of a social geography, recalling Henri Lefebvre's notion of the "social production of space," which was seminal for the Situationist International, brings us to the alienating nature of urban public spaces.

THE CITY OF POWER

The city is a privileged space where socioeconomic powers exert their most obvious control and influence; where dominant ideologies are everywhere reinforced and resisted. Urban space reflects social and racial inequalities, and it is undeniably gendered.

As Janet Wolff pointed out, "The literature of modernity describes the experience of men." [53] In the nineteenth century, the *flâneuse* could never be simply the feminine pendant of the *flâneur*. A woman roaming the public spaces of the modern city was a *fille publique*, a lost woman, a prostitute working the streets in search of a client. The modern city was represented from a male point of view, as a leisure/spectacle society, where men were the customers and women the consumed in their roles as workers of the leisure industry—barmaids, singers, dancers, acrobats, prostitutes, and so forth. As Griselda Pollock puts it: "Women did not enjoy the freedom of incognito in the crowd. They were never positioned as the normal occupants of the public realm. They did not have the right to look, to stare, scrutinize or watch. As the Baudelairean text goes on to show, women do not look. They are positioned as the *object* of the flâneur's gaze." [54] The public spaces of the modern city were the sites where male writers and artists developed the aesthetic of modernity, while the "respectable" woman's experience, still confined to private, domestic spaces, was excluded. Only with the opening

Ilona Granet, *Curb Your Animal Instinct*, 1986

of the first department stores in the mid-nineteenth century did middle-class women appear in the public sphere—but the strolling woman was then essentially a consumer, her visibility a sign of her husband's social standing.[55]

In recent years, women's exclusion from the public realm has been questioned by artists who commented on the female experience in the gendered spaces of postmodern life. In Yoko Ono's film *Rape*, as the title indicates, the following of women takes on a totally different connotation from that in Vito Acconci's *Following Piece* or Sophie Calle's *The Shadow*. *Rape*, along with Ilona Granet's *Curb Your Animal Instinct* (1986) or *No Cat Calls* (1987), evokes women's experience in public urban spaces through a critique of the male coveting gaze, all too often synonymous with intrusion and harassment.

Urban social geography can also be traced back to the nineteenth century. Reflecting on Benjamin's view of that period as the prehistory of modernity, Susan Buck-Morss wrote: "As Ur-forms of contemporary life, Benjamin avoided more obvious social types and went to the margins. He singled out the *flâneur*, [the] prostitute...."[56] One might add to this citation of the marginalized the homeless person who dwells between the city walls, whom Benjamin evokes in the context of his metaphors of the street as interior, describing a bag lady lying under a bridge in Paris, with her belongings gathered around her as if to create "the shadow of an interior." [57]

The recurrent metaphors of urban dislocation, disorientation, and nomadism in Benjamin's *Passagen-Werk*, which go back to what Georg Lukacs called the "transcendental homelessness" of the modern world and Kracauer's "existential topography" of transcience,[58] conjure up essential aspects of the alienating urban experience.[59]

Under Napoleon III, Paris underwent a drastic transformation. In order to build new boulevards, Baron Haussmann destroyed the old city. The Paris we know today is the result of radical changes wrought by its "Haussmannization," when the slums inhabited by the street sellers, organ grinders, ragpickers, and other urban nomads who had roamed the streets of the city since the Middle Ages were destroyed and their inhabitants expelled to the *banlieue*. This phenomenon did not escape the attention of the painters of modern life. Among the artistic bohemia, Daumier, Manet, Raffaelli, and

Adrian Piper, *Catalysis*, 1970–72

later Picasso (in his Blue and Rose periods) devoted much interest to the city's nomad outcasts.

Contemporary artists express a similar concern for the socially and economically inflicted nomadism in our post-industrial cities, namely, homelessness.[60] The urban historian Mike Davis has pointed out that the privatization of urban public spaces in Los Angeles has resulted in the ostracization of street life. The pedestrian is reduced to opprobrium and the homeless nomad to banishment. Relegated to the "outdoor poorhouse" of Skid Row, the homeless are regarded as undesirable, useless human beings, an attitude that testifies to blind capitalist exploitation and inadequate, inhuman social politics.[61] In New York, as Rosalyn Deutsche has argued, "uneven economic and geographical development is a structural, rather than incidental, feature of New York's present expansion," [62] since space is produced by and reproduces social relations.[63]

The gentrification of New York or Los Angeles, reminiscent of the Haussmannization of Paris, implies abandonment and the exclusion of the urban poor. Hans Haacke's *Shapolsky et al. Manhattan Real Estate Holdings, a Real Time Social System, as of May 1, 1971*, documents the systematic exploitation, for private profit, of the largest concentration of real estate owned by a single group—slums and vacant lots located on the Lower East Side and in Harlem.[64] And Francesc Torres, in his video *Belchite-South Bronx: A Trans-Historical, Trans-Cultural Landscape* (1987-88), shows a devastating parallel between the effects of real-estate speculation and bombings during wartime.

The resulting experience of dislocation and alienation is expressed by Adrian Piper in her performance *Catalysis* (1970-72). Piper roamed the city streets and public transportation systems dressed and smelling like a bag lady—a reiteration of the *dérive* trope with a dose of socially charged criticism that comments very directly on the homeless condition. During Tehching Hsieh's *One Year Performance*, from September 26, 1981, to September 26, 1982, he lived in the streets, never entering a building except when he was arrested by the police, an event documented on videotape. Hsieh's action bridges the gap between, on the one hand, the obsolete deliberate attitudes of intellectual and artistic bohemians or *flâneurs*, the

51

revolutionary zeal of Situationist unitary urbanism and psychogeographical *dérive*, and, on the other, the tragic alienation of the homeless nomads roaming the city. Also commenting on urban estrangement, David Hammons' *Bliz-aard Ball Sale* (1983) is a very poignant—desperate—icon of the adverse face of consumer society and those it excludes. Among her statements on this society, Jenny Holzer's site-specific *Truisms* were meant to intermittently flash shocking statements such as: "Abuse of power comes as no surprise," on the walls of the city. Martha Rosler has devoted much attention to the problem of homelessness, in exhibitions such as "Homeless: The Street and Other Venues" or her book *If You Lived Here: The City in Art, Theory, and Social Activism*,[65] while Dan Wiley analyzed the uneven development of New York in *The Two Waterfronts* (1989).

Among recent endeavors to interact with the homeless people, improve their situation, and heighten public awareness of their plight are Krzysztof Wodiczko's *New Museum Projection* (1991), which addresses the housing crisis, and his *Homeless Vehicle* (1989). In these works, he creates public "monuments" dedicated to a shocking reality that is usually carefully kept out of sight. In so doing, the artist inverts the role expected of public art by revealing, instead of suppressing, the contradictions and conflicts of interest inherent to urban space. [66]

Tehching Hsieh,
One Year Perfomance, 1981–82

Notes

1. Charles Baudelaire, "The Heroism of Modern Life," in *Art in Paris 1845-1862: Salons and Other Exhibitions Reviewed by Charles Baudelaire*, transl. Jonathan Mayne (Oxford: Phaidon Press, 1965), pp.118-19.

2. Ibid., p.119.

3. Charles Baudelaire, *The Painter of Modern Life and Other Essays*, transl. Jonathan Mayne (New York: Da Capo Press, 1964), p.13.

4. Quoted in Maurice Nadeau, *Histoire dusurréalisme* (Paris: Éditions du Seuil, 1964), p.28, from Baudelaire's "Salon de 1859."

5. Isabelle Monod-Fontaine (ed.), *André Breton: La beauté convulsive*, exhibition catalogue (Paris: Musée National d'Art Moderne, 1991), p.106.

6. For Max Morise's comments on the group's insufficient awareness of the limitations of chance and the failure of this open-country, intercity excursion to yield excitement, see Jean-Hubert Martin, "Dérives," in *Cartes et figures de la terre*, exhibition catalogue (Paris: Musée National d'Art Moderne, 1980), p.197, quoting from Morise in *La révolution surréaliste*, no.11 (March 15, 1928), p.1. Morise's criticism was later quoted verbatim (as usual without source) by Guy Debord in "Theory of the Dérive," *Internationale Situationniste*, no. 2 (December 1958), in Ken Knabb, ed., *Situationist International Anthology* (Berkeley: Bureau of Public Secrets, 1981), p.51.

7. *André Breton: La beauté convulsive*, p.170.

8. Louis Aragon, *Nightwalker*, transl. Frederick Brown (Englewood Cliffs, New Jersey: Prentice Hall, 1970), p.9

9. In Walter Benjamin, *Reflections*, transl. Harry Zohn (New York: Schocken Books, 1986), pp. 178-83.

10. See Rolf Tiedemann's introduction to Walter Benjamin, *Das Passagen-Werk* (Frankfurt: Suhrkamp Verlag, 1983), I, p.17 and passim.

11. Burkhardt Lindner, "The *Passagen-Werk*, the *Berliner Kindheit*, and the Archaeology of the 'Recent Past,'" *New German Critique*, no. 39 (Fall 1986), pp. 26-27. On "spatial reification," see also Anthony Vidler, "Agoraphobia: Spatial Estrangement in Simmel and Kracauer," *New German Critique*, no. 54 (Fall 1991), pp.31-45.

12. Walter Benjamin, "Der Flaneur," *Das Passagen-Werk*, I, pp.525 [M 1,4], 531 [M 3,1], [M 3,2], 532 [M 3,4], 533 [M 3a,4], 537 [M 5,1]. Also "Pariser Passagen II," II, pp.1051-52: "The collective is an eternally alert, eternally moving being that witnesses, experiences, perceives and devises as much between the house walls outside as individuals within the protection of their own walls. To the collective, the shining enameled signs of a store company are just as good as or better than the decorative oil paintings on the wall of the bourgeois salon. Walls with the sign 'Défense d'afficher' are the collective's writing desk, newspaper stands its libraries, mailboxes its bronze sculptures, benches its bedroom furnishings, and the café terraces are the alcoves from which it looks down at its home. Where the asphalt worker lets his coat hang on the railing, that is the vestibule. And the gateway, leading out into the open from multiple court yards is the long corridor which frightens the bourgeois; but it is to them the entrance into the chambers of the city. For them, the arcade (*passage*) was the salon. It is in the arcade, more so than in any other place, that the street reveals its identity as the masses' furnished, lived-in interior."

13. See Burkhardt Lindner, "The *Passagen-Werk*," pp.34-36. The parallel between city and apartment calls to mind Benjamin's contemporary, the Dadaist Kurt Schwitters, who filled his Hannover apartment with found materials and objects brought in from the city. The resulting Merzbau-apartment evokes

the city as labyrinth described by Benjamin; see "Der Flaneur," *Das Passagen-Werk*, I, p.541 [M 6a,4].

14. The history and meaning of spaces was formulated in the cultural analyses of critics such as Theodor Adorno, Siegfried Kracauer, Georg Simmel, Walter Benjamin, Henri Lefebvre, Michel Foucault, Paul Virilio, Griselda Pollock, Janet Wolff, and others.

15. Svetlana Alpers, "The Mapping Impulse in Dutch Art," *The Art of Describing: Dutch Art in the Seventeenth Century* (Chicago: University of Chicago Press, 1983), pp.119-68, describes a process of topological mapping of landscape in the Low Countries which differed from the Albertian perspectival system of illusionism practiced in Italy, according to which the world was depicted as if seen through a window. In topological mapping, several points of view overlap to produce a comprehensive "description" of the landscape, as if in a bird's-eye view. This multiplication of viewpoints, in addition to fragmentation and the use of symbolic rather than iconic signs, is also what differentiates Cubism from the Western tradition of illusionism; see Yve-Alain Bois, "Kahnweiler's Lesson," in *Painting as Model* (Cambridge, Massachusetts: The MIT Press, 1990), pp.65-97.

16. Rosalind Krauss, "Grids," in *The Originality of the Avant-Garde and Other Modernist Myths* (Cambridge, Massachusetts: The MIT Press, 1986), pp.8-22.

17. Yve-Alain Bois, *Painting as Model*, p.182, quoting from Leo Steinberg, "Other Criteria," in *Other Criteria: Confrontations with Twentieth-Century Art* (New York: Oxford University Press, 1972), p.88.

18. Michel de Certeau, *The Practices of Everyday Life*, transl. Steven Rendall (Berkeley and Los Angeles, California: University of California Press, 1988), p.93.

19. Fredric Jameson, "The Cultural Logic of Late Capitalism," (1984), in *Postmodernism, or The Cultural Logic of Late Capitalism* (Durham, North Carolina: Duke University Press, 1991).

20. Benjamin, "Der Flaneur," *Das Passagen-Werk*, I, p.524, quoting from Marcel Reja, *L'art chez les fous* (1907), p.131.

21. *Internationale Situationniste*, no.1 (June 1958), p.5; see Peter Wollen, "From Breton to Situationism," *New Left Review*, no.174, p.77.

22. Essay published in the first issue of *Internationale Situationniste* (p.19), in Knabb, *Situationist International Anthology*, p.3.

23. "Our central idea," wrote Guy Debord, "is that of the construction of situations, that is to say, the concrete construction of momentary ambiances of life and their transformation into a superior pas-

sional quality"; in "Report on the Construction of Situations and on the International Situationist Tendency's Conditions of Organization and Action," in Knabb, *Situationist International Anthology*, p.22.

24. This idea is explained in Jean-François Martos, *Histoire de l'Internationale Situationniste* (Paris: Éditions Gérard Lebovici, 1989), pp.18-19.

25. Guy-Ernest Debord, "Introduction to a Critique of Urban Geography" (1955), in Knabb, *Situationist International Anthology*, p.7. The translation used here is from *On the Passage of a Few People Through a Rather Brief Moment in Time: The Situationist International 1957-1972*, exhibition catalogue (Boston: Institute of Contemporary Art, 1989), p.139, note 3.

26. Translated in *On The Passage of a Few People Through a Rather Brief Moment in Time*, p.138, from Guy-Ernest Debord, "Théorie de la dérive," *Les lévres nues*, 9 (November 1956), pp.10-13.

27. Wollen, "The Situationist International," pp.80-82.

28. Quoted in Martos, *Histoire de l'Internationale Situationiste*, p.26.

29. George Maciunas, "Fluxus Manifesto" (1963), in Clive Phillpot and Jon Hendricks, *Fluxus: Selections from the Gilbert and Lila Silverman Collection*, exhibition catalogue (New York: The Museum of Modern Art, 1988), frontispiece.

30. Conversation with Benjamin Patterson, March 25, 1992. The invitation was designed by Benjamin Patterson, printed by George Maciunas, and later edited for spelling by Robert Filliou.

31. *Potlach*, no.1, quoted by Debord in "Introduction to a Critique of Urban Geography," in Knabb, *Situationist International Anthology*, p.6.

32. Yoko Ono, *Grapefruit: A Book of Instructions by Yoko Ono* (New York: Simon and Schuster, 1970).

33. In 1959, the Dutch Situationists planned to transform the Stedelijk Museum in Amsterdam into a labyrinth. The mini-*dérive* organized on these restricted premises was to correspond to a radio-guided *dérive* through Amsterdam—but the whole project was ultimately canceled; see Martos, *Histoire de l'Internationale Situationniste*, p.128.

34. *Douglas Huebler*, exhibition catalogue (New York: Seth Siegelaub, 1968), no.7.

35. Debord, "Théorie de la dérive" (1958), in Knabb, *Situationist International Anthology*, pp.50-54.

36. Conversation with the artist, February 28, 1992.

37. Quoted in Knabb, *Situationist International Anthology*, p.50.

38. Similarly Andy Warhol's real-time film *Empire* (1964), which consists of a stable image of the

building, filmed from a unique point of view, during a twenty-four hour period, and merely records changes of light, is a critique of Albertian illusionism, all the more puzzling when applied to the film medium because it reveals more about time than about space. It is an eloquent satire on the alleged possibility of representation equaling real time and real space. Warhol's film echoes Dziga Vertov's *The Man with the Movie Camera* (1928), where he filmed a large city, from dawn to night, without actors, script, or scenario; see Martos, *Histoire de l'Internationale Situationniste*, p.33.

39. See Rudi H. Fuchs, *Discordance/Cohérence* (Eindhoven: Stedelijk Van Abbemuseum, 1976), p.4.

40. The seven successive locations were: Chinatown, East Village, Greenwich Village, Times Square, Soho, Central Park, and Wall Street; ibid., pp.54-56.

41. Debord, "Théorie de la dérive" (1958) in Knabb, *Situationist International Anthology*, pp.52-53.

42. Paul Virilio, "The Overexposed City," in *The Lost Dimension*, transl. Daniel Moshenberg (New York: Semiotext[e], 1991), p.18.

43. Benjamin, "Der Flâneur," *Das Passagen-Werk* I, p.532 [M 3,8].

44. Virilio, "The Overexposed City," p.21.

45. These locations, in and around Paris, were: Forêt de Saint-Germain, Parc des Buttes-Chaumont, Jardin des Plantes, Lac intérieur du Bois de Boulogne, Parc zoologique du Bois de Vincennes, Service Conservation de la Nature, Collection de Minéralogie de l'Ecole des Mines, Musée de l'Assistance Publique, Passage du Caire; see Martin, "Dérives," pp.197-202. Martin also mentions Robert Longo, whose extra-urban *dérives*, along with those of Robert Smithson, fall outside the parameters of this exhibition.

46. See John Rignall, "Benjamin's *Flâneur* and the Problem of Realism," in Andrew Benjamin, ed., *The Problems of Modernity: Adorno and Benjamin* (London and New York: Routledge, 1989), pp.116-19.

47. What is at play in the above-mentioned instances of *dérive* is not influence but intertextuality, which means that, as Fredric Jameson puts it (writing about film), the "awareness of the preexistence of other versions [is seen as] constitutive and essential..."—intertextuality being "a deliberate, built-in feature of the aesthetic effect"; Jameson, "The Cultural Logic of Late Capitalism" (1984), in *Postmodernism*, p.20.

48. *Arman 1955-1991: A Retrospective*, exhibition catalogue (Houston: The Museum of Fine Arts, 1991), p.120.

49. Jameson, "The Cultural Logic of Late Capitalism," p.15.

50. Ibid.

51. Ibid., p.51.

52. Ibid., p.52.

53. Janet Wolff, "The Invisible *Flâneuse*: Women and the Literature of Modernity," in *The Problems of Modernity*, p.141.

54. Griselda Pollock, "Modernity and the Spaces of Femininity," in *Vision and Difference: Femininity, Feminism and Histories of Art* (London and New York: Routledge, 1988), p.71.

55. Wolff, "The Invisible *Flâneuse*," p.153.

56. Susan Buck-Morss, "The Flâneur, the Sandwichman, and the Whore: The Politics of Loitering," *New German Critique*, no.39 (Fall 1986), p.101.

57. Benjamin, *Das Passagen-Werk*, I, p.537 [M 5,1]; quoting from Marcel Jouhandeau, *Images de Paris* (Paris, 1934), p.62.

58. Vidler, "Agoraphobia," passim.

59. Tiedemann, in Benjamin, *Das Passagen-Werk*, II, p.1215: "Dialectic of Flânerie: The interior as street (luxury)/the street as interior (misery)."

60. In this sense, their endeavor, rather than epitomize postmodern art, establishes a continuity with a modernist avant-garde which is too often systematically positioned as the incarnation of a Kantian autonomy of culture and aesthetics.

61. Mike Davis, *City of Quartz: Excavating the Future in Los Angeles* (London and New York: Verso, 1990), passim.

62. Rosalyn Deutsche,"Uneven Development: Public Art in New York City," *October*, no.47 (Winter 1988), p.4.

63. Henri Lefebvre has demonstrated this point in *The Production of Social Space* (1974), transl. Donald Nicholson-Smith (Oxford and Cambridge, Massachusetts: Blackwell, 1991).

64. See *Hans Haacke: Unfinished Business*, exhibition catalogue (New York: The New Museum of Contemporary Art, 1986); especially Rosalyn Deutsche's essay "Property Value: Hans Haacke, Real Estate, and the Museum," pp.20-37.

65. Brian Wallis, ed., *If You Lived Here: The City in Art, Theory, and Social Activism. A Project by Martha Rosler* (Seattle: Bay Press, 1991).

66. Deutsche, "Uneven Development," p.52. She considers *The Homeless Vehicle* as an example of Situationist *détournement*—"the interpretation of present or past artistic productions into a superior construction of a milieu"; see *Internationale Situationniste*, no.1 (June 1958), p.13.

THE URBAN EVENT:
SPECTACLE, RESISTANCE, AND HEGEMONY

Karen Jones

A rebellion against the spectacle is situated on the level of *totality* because—even if it were to appear in the single district of Watts—it is a protest of people against inhuman life; because it begins at the level of the *real single individual* and because community, from which the rebelling individual is separated, is the *true social nature* of man, human nature: the positive supersession of the spectacle.

—*Internationale Situationniste*, 1965 [1]

THE LETTRIST JOURNAL *Potlatch* takes its name from the practice of Native American tribes whereby "one chief met another and offered gifts. The second chief had to respond in kind, but on a higher plane of value. That was the potlatch. The game might begin with the presentation of a necklace and end with the burning of a town—with a tribe burning its own town, thus raising the obligations of its rival to an almost impossible level." [2]

The ritual of potlatch disrupts the notion of materialism as a sanctified value structure and raises the destruction of property to an act of communal social exchange/negotiation value; thereby dismissing claims to private ownership and the privilege of the material (commodity) object. Marcel Mauss, in Greil Marcus' summary, theorized the potlatch as a "negation of division, as an affirmation of community. It was, [Mauss] said, the first round table from which none need be excluded—or could be." [3] Therefore, the potlatch and the riot have similar attributes in that both are instances based on shared community interests. The riot is a direct response to an action, policy, or social condition which threatens or challenges the collectively identified interests of the resisting subjects.

In the Situationist document "The Decline and Fall of the Spectacle-Commodity Economy," an astute analysis of the 1965 Watts Riots is made in terms of the mass rejection of the conditions of commodification and

David Wojnarowicz, *Arthur Rimbaud in New York*, 1978-1979

the African-American participation in a "potlatch of destruction." The Watts Riots manifested "a rebellion against the commodity, against the world of the commodity in which worker-consumers are *hierarchically* subordinated to commodity values."[4] The participants of the Watts Riots claimed and "consumed" property in order to dominate and displace the socially inscribed value of the commodity object.

The forces opposing each other during the act of riot are the masses and what Louis Althusser refers to as the "Repressive State Apparatus" (RSA): "the State Apparatus in question *functions by violence*"; it exists as a monolithic structure and includes "the Government, the Administration, the Army, the Police, the Courts, the Prisons...."[5]

The Situationists developed and practiced unitary urbanism, a "theory of the combined use of arts and techniques for the integral construction of a milieu in dynamic relation with experiments in behavior."[6] Unitary urbanism constructs a location for cultural practice within an urban environment to challenge dominant systems of power through a theoretical model. There is an operative political strategy embedded within the agenda to produce "situations and experimental models of possible modes of transformation of the city, as well as to agitate and polemicize against the sterility and oppression of the actual environment and ruling economic and political system."[7] The merger of art practice and social behavior politicizes the events within daily routine and everyday existence.

In the series *Arthur Rimbaud in New York* (1978-79), David Wojnarowicz depicts his aleatory drifts through the cityscape. He makes an emotional

link among alienation, homelessness, and dislocation with photographs that document actual meanderings through urban haunts—places which resonate with personal, lived experience. In this sense, the series makes reference to the Situationist concept of the *dérive*, "a mode of experimental behavior linked to the conditions of urban society: a technique of transient passage through varied ambiances." [8] The *Rimbaud* series creates a locatable contemporary reference to the actual lived conditions of the (discarded) subjects of the postindustrial urban space.

At the time that he produced the *Arthur Rimbaud* photographs, Wojnarowicz had just returned to New York from Paris. The series addresses his subsequent displacement in the American urban environment through revisits to locations within city and mental space. Wojnarowicz documents his emotional reference to sites both within the urban landscape and within his sensory memory: the piers, graffiti-covered warehouse walls, Times Square, subway cars, Coney Island, a coffee shop, a bar—locations that allude to the interstitial moments within everyday life. Wojnarowicz fuses experiment and survival, creating a space for the *dérive* born of the social condition which constitutes a politically conscious subject. Of the psychogeography within the *Rimbaud* series Wojnarowicz writes:

> I was young, broke and feeling that I was close to living on the streets again....I fashioned a mask of Rimbaud and brought him on a narrative trail that touched my biographical past—the places I haunted when living on the streets in my teens as well as the industrial sites that were like technological meadows where I could place new york city to my back.

I didn't think I would survive another bout of living on the streets and with some borrowed dollars wanted to create a body of work that could survive me and speak of locations and movements that had attracted me to that point. I didn't see myself as Rimbaud but rather used him as a device to confront my own desires, experiences, biography and to try and touch on those elusive "sites of attraction"; those places that suddenly and unexpectedly revive the smell and traces of former states of body and mind long ago left behind....I was also attracted to the "youth" in the series; the rock n roll do or die abandon of that period of time. [9]

GRAFFITI AND AFTER

Graffiti artists riding the New York subways in the early 1980s recod[ed] the balloonlike lettering of Disney comics into gigantesque and magical writings of their own names as signs of a new-found personal freedom....

—Rosalind Krauss [10]

The graffiti movement is located at the intersection of public space as a site for representation and the alienation resulting from a marginalized and "outlawed" existence. During the period 1971-82, urban youth claimed the city landscape—the streets, subway stations, and subway cars—reclaiming these public spaces as available and accessible sites for representation.[11] Issues such as the right to public space and access to the systems of cultural validation emerged as a result of this subcultural practice and consequently curtailed the impact of the graffiti movement. The transit authorities (RSA) mounted a mass crackdown on both the representations and the "writers" through legislation prohibiting the sale of spray paint to minors, to arrests and killings, and finally to the institution of "buff," a chemical substance which protected the surface of the trains.

The graffiti artists utilized public space both to comment on access to elite institutions and as a means of rupturing social order. The practice has a transgressive effect in that it claims space in order to gain status; this status is then challenged, resisted, and ultimately depoliticized by the hegemonic

Jean-Michel Basquiat,
The Bond, Earle or Stanhope, 1982

Jean-Michel Basquiat and Al Diaz,
frame from *New York Beat,* 1981

Jean-Michel Basquiat,
graffiti from *SAMO,* 1982

forces within the City of Power. The art world further exploited the graffiti movement by taking the works out of context and offering them as a commodity, displacing and coopting the original form of expression, which served to further fragment the cultural practice. "Graffiti is largely mediated," wrote Hal Foster, "even on the streets it has become its own reified ritual....Rather than circulate against the code, graffiti is now mostly fixed by it: a form of access to it, not a transgression of it....graffiti art is concerned less to contest the lines between museum and margin, high and low, than to find a place within them.[12]

Artists in the graffiti movement gained recognition through their individual "tags"—signature styles, which are documented in piece books. Crash, Daze, Futura 2000, Lee, Lady Pink, Phase 2, Stash, Toxic, and Rammellzee, among others, established their reputations through emblematic murals that emblazoned subway trains and urban street walls.

The SAMO (Same Old Shit) project of Jean-Michel Basquiat and Al Diaz employed the techniques and vocabulary of the graffiti movement, but their work specifically addressed the art world. In locating their texts and dialogue directly in the geographical urban space of the art trade—the East Village and SoHo/Tribeca—they presented a critique of the hegemonic forces within the art world. Serial spray paint writings and drawings appeared on city walls with phases such as "THE WHOLE LIVERY LINE BOW LIKE THIS WITH THE BIG MONEY ALL CRUSHED INTO..."—open challenges to the art system from the street.

Basquiat's painting *The Bond, Earle or Stanhope* (1982) depicts three New York City hotels on canvas; sections of the stretcher bars remain exposed. The class stratifications of the urban environment are mapped through the juxtaposition of three different classes of hotels that are unable to be accommodated by the confines of the established picture plane. The canvas (as city space) cannot meet the structure of the stretchers, which lays bare the structural class fragmentation and collision evidenced within both the representation and experience of the postmodern city.

Gary Simmons' figurative sculpture *Everlast Champion* (1991) consists of two pairs of gold-plated high-top sneakers wall mounted on plexiglass shelves (displayed). Simmons' sculpture comments specifically on identity

Gary Simmons, *Everlast Champion,* 1991

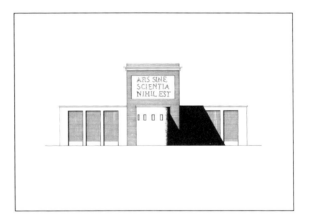

Aldo Rossi, *South Bronx Academy of Art*, 1991
(South and North Elevations)

within hip-hop, an urban, primarily African-American culture, which is an outgrowth of the phenomena of graffiti, break dancing, and rap. The high-top sneaker emerged as a status emblem among alienated urban youth; violent incidents including murders occurred over these commodity objects. The status value of the sneakers was reinforced by advertising campaigns aimed at the urban minority youth market. Simmons' *Everlast Champion* uses gold-plate as a trope for the commodity fetish, which becomes a site of contention for displaced rage vis-á-vis the commodity spectacle (*Everlast Champion*).

Aldo Rossi's design for the South Bronx Academy of Art (1991) is a commission for Tim Rollins & K.O.S. The projected Academy, an outgrowth of the Art & Knowledge Workshop, will consist of an elaborate building with a colonnade leading to a lighthouse structure (beacon), a courtyard, and a school building (including art studios, lecture halls, and gallery spaces). The South Bronx Academy of Art project aims to establish an institution within the disenfranchised inner city sphere in order to offer a positive alternative to inadequate educational options. Rollins utilizes both the urban site and the urban social condition as loci for a model of intervention designed to resist the socioeconomic disparities that determine unequal education along race/class lines.

THE RIOT

The political scientist Richard Foglesong defines the capitalist-democracy contradiction: "Democracy naturalizes individualistic conceptions of human beings and, as Marx maintained, by falsely dividing the political and private spheres, it legitimates the structure of domination inherent in the private property relation." [13]

Andy Warhol's *Birmingham Race Riot* (1964) (re)presents the mass-circulated media image of an event in Birmingham, Alabama, in May 1963. Policemen turned their (RSA) attack dogs on the participants of a non-violent anti-segregation demonstration. The original photograph appeared in *Life* as a document of the police brutality leveled against civil rights activists and workers. "Rather than simply continuing the circulation of mass-media icons, the works are projected as operating in a self-conscious denaturing of these icons that makes them, on some level, critical of late capitalism."[14]

Warhol's *Birmingham Race Riot*, through repetitive, mechanically reproduced images, depicts the harsh evidence of social/racial conflict in a bold graphic format. Simultaneously, it comments on the dissemination of this imagery as product within the context of both popular (publishing) and fine art cultures as contemporaneously serving commodity interests. *Birmingham Race Riot* speaks directly of the conflicts produced and escalated within a system of oppression on race/class lines, (re)presenting the savagery and brutality located within the City of Power.

Historically, the term "riot" has been erroneously used to denote a state of disorder, chaos, and upheaval with no fundamental organization or causal relationship to specific events or to the oppression located within social systems. I use the term here as synonymous with uprising, event, rebellion, or revolutionary moment. The concept foregrounds a renegotiation of power linked specifically to the social/political intent invested within the act of riot. The riot is a logical consequence of the oppressive forces within the capitalist modern and postmodern space.[15]

The act of resistance marks a moment when the unconscious becomes conscious and challenges an existing social order. The internalized oppression becomes externalized and thereby stakes a claim, within the public domain, through the demonstration of rage and violence.[16]

The urban riot locates a site of contestation. It is an event which signifies struggle and resistance as redress to social grievances. The riot materializes either spontaneously, as when a peaceful demonstration is provoked by police brutality, or through organized aggressive action. The riot as a political and social action threatens and disrupts social order. It usurps and activates "public space." Each riot involves an underlying class conflict that is often coded by issues of race relations, labor conditions, and systematic poverty. I will discuss one instance of the urban event, the Tompkins Square Park Riot, in order illustrate the class struggle articulated within this specific uprising.

Andy Warhol, detail of *Birmingham Race Riot*, 1964

The Tompkins Square Riot of August 6, 1988, marked a significant conflict among the many forces generated by the political and economic structure of the postmodern, postindustrial urban site. The underlying issue was the gentrification of the East Village and the Lower East Side of Manhattan. The plan of gentrification involved mass capital investment in an urban renewal project which would transform a lower working-class neighborhood into a community for the professional labor forces of the financial district and the World Trade Center. "Rather than a stage in an inevitable progression of urban growth, redevelopment was, throughout the 1980s, a comprehensive transformation of the environment driven by the need to facilitate capital accumulation and enhance state control."[17] This process began in the East Village in 1980 along the west side of Tompkins Square Park.[18]

The emergence of the East Village art scene, which began in 1981, further increased the cachet of the area, forcing up rents and displacing longtime residents. As Rosalyn Deutsche and Cara Gendel Ryan observed, "The representation of the Lower East Side as an 'adventurous avant-garde setting,' however, conceals a brutal reality. For the site of this brave new art scene is also a strategic urban arena where the city, financed by big capital, wages its war of position against an impoverished and increasingly isolated local population."[19]

Eventually, the forces within the newly gentrified East Village came into an open conflict. As a direct result of gentrification, the homeless population of Tompkins Square Park steadily increased, and by 1988 there were as many as three hundred evicted homeless people who had taken up residence in the park. Community groups complained of the condition of the park, and the authorities dredged up a long-forgotten ordinance that required the park to close at 1am in order to clear the homeless population from this public space. [20]

On August 6, 1988, there was a demonstration consisting of about "100 punks, students, local residents, activists, squatters, and homeless people convened in the evening in Tompkins Square Park, committed to preventing the police from enforcing the 1am curfew and taking back the park. There were a number of chants: 'Gentrification is genocide.' 'Die Yuppie Scum'…'Class War.' 'Yuppies and real estate magnates have declared war on the people of

Tompkins Square Park.'" [21] This organized resistance was generated by a community of subjects who sought to maintain "public space."

It is within the context of the struggle between the newly arrived "gentry" served by the police (RSA) and the homeless who claimed right of access to public space that the violent uprising materialized. The organized resistance to the reclaiming of the park was met by authorities with brutal force. An eyewitness account reported "the cops seemed bizarrely out of control....They'd taken a relatively small protest and fanned it out over the neighborhood, inflaming hundreds of people....[There were] cavalry charges down East Village streets, a chopper circling overhead, people out for a Sunday paper running in terror down First Avenue." [22]

Krzysztof Wodiczko's *The Homeless Vehicle* (1989) addresses the prevalence of homelessness as a direct effect of gentrification and its broader link to the global restructuring of capital accumulation in a technology-based economy. The vehicle, which serves as a mobile shelter and collection apparatus, does not seek to solve the housing problem but instead recognizes the homeless condition: human beings (a population) caught in the web of societal restructuring along class lines: "When in the capitalist city residents are no longer required in the economy, a condition observable in the homeless populations of today's restructured cities, the need for those residents and for the conditions of their survival—capital's social needs —disappears." [23] The victims of this restructuring are left without prospects for employment or housing. "To some degree," Wodiczko has noted, "those people are the nomads in historic ways, but the context is completely different. They are born of transformation of the city....It means that the contemporary nomad will always be on the edge of everything and will be in conflict with everyone." [24]

In Wodiczko's lightbox installation *New York City Tableaux: Tompkins Square* (1988), military equipment and language are superimposed over photographs of the homeless in Tompkins Square Park in order to insist upon political empowerment for the postmodern nomad. Texts such as "EVICTS OF ALL CITIES, UNITE!" expand the Tompkins Square Park condition (local) to a global framework.

David Hammons' installation *Cold Shoulders* (1990) depicts the home-

David Hammons, *Cold Shoulders,* 1990

Krzysztof Wodiczko, *The Homeless Vehicle,* 1989

Barbara Kruger, *Untitled (Questions),* 1991

Tony Cokes, frame from *Black Celebration,* 1988

less subject(s) by presenting three human-scale ice blocks shoulder-wrapped in overcoats. The ice blocks eventually melt in an ironic reference to the many homeless who have frozen to death in the urban streets and parks.[25] Thus, the unsheltered are ignored by the agents of power (the cold shoulder) who have little interest in the displaced evictees of the urban center. At the intersection of the social conditions imposed by the Power of the City and the blanket refusal of the government (RSA) to remedy these conditions lies a political space.

Barbara Kruger's *Untitled (Questions)* (1991) addresses the art world at a strategic site: the closed city gate of the Mary Boone Gallery. Kruger breaks the confines of the interior gallery setting in order to publicly address the political issues at stake—the sources of class conflict. Kruger locates the viewer's position with pointed political questions: "Look for the moment when pride becomes contempt. Who is free to choose? Who is beyond the law? Who is healed? Who is housed? Who speaks? Who is silenced?" Kruger rhetorically questions who, what class, is accommodated within the structures of urban American late capitalism.

The Tony Cokes video *Black Celebration* (1988) utilizes documentary footage of the 1960s riots of Watts, Newark, Detroit, and Boston, all of which were clearly linked to racial oppression. Cokes combines Situationist texts, Barbara Kruger's writings, and industrial rock music to foreground the anarchistic content invested and articulated within the urban event. *Black Celebration* addresses the sociopolitical and economic conflicts expressed within the dialectic of resistance and oppression, as represented and circulated within the realm of mass media as a form of social documentary. The newsreel documentation historicizes the riots by revealing the consequent eruption of rage produced by and located within the phenomenon of the contemporary capitalist urban space.

In the analysis of the urban event it is crucial to consider acts of resistance that do not result in aggressive confrontations as considerable gestures in relationship to the hegemonic forces contained within the City of Power. "And hegemony has the advantage over general notions of totality, that it at the same time emphasizes the facts of domination."[26] The art practices discussed here are resistant and informative gestures which reclaim agency for individual subjects, as the oppressive realities imposed by the postmodern city increasingly reshape and dehumanize the urban site.

Notes

1. Quoted in Ken Knabb, ed., *Situationist International Anthology* (Berkeley: Bureau of Public Secrets, 1981), pp.159-60.

2. Greil Marcus, *Lipstick Traces: A Secret History of the Twentieth Century* (Cambridge, Massachusetts: Harvard University Press, 1989), p.393.

3. Ibid., p.394.

4. Quoted in Knabb, *Situationist International Anthology*, p.155.

5. Louis Althusser, "Ideology and Ideological State Apparatuses (Notes toward an Investigation)," in *Lenin and Philosophy and Other Essays*, transl. Ben Brewster (New York and London: Monthly Review Press, 1969), pp.143-44.

6. Quoted in Knabb, *Situationist International Anthology*, p.45.

7. Peter Wollen, "The Art and Politics of Situationist International," in *On the Passage of a Few People Through a Rather Brief Moment in Time: The Situationist International, 1957-1972*, exhibition catalogue (Boston: Institute of Contemporary Art, 1989), p.22.

8. Quoted in Knabb, *Situationist International Anthology*, p.45.

9. David Wojnarowicz, unpublished manuscript, November 1990, New York.

10. Rosalind Krauss, "Nostalgie de la Boue," *October*, no.56 (Spring 1991), p.115.

11. Martha Cooper and Henry Chalfant, *Subway Art* (New York: Henry Holt, 1984), pp.5-17.

12. Hal Foster,"Between Modernism and the Media," *Recodings: Art, Spectacle, Cultural Politics* (Seattle: Bay Press, 1985), pp.51-52.

13. As summarized in Rosalyn Deutsche, "Alternative Space," in Brian Wallis, ed., *If You Lived Here: The City in Art, Theory, and Social Activism. A Project by Martha Rosler* (Seattle: Bay Press, 1991), p.59.

14. David Evans, "The Unsecret Life: A Warhol Advertisement," *October*, no.56 (Spring 1991), p.27.

15. The ideas in this paragraph reflect conversations with Ron Clark, February 1992.

16. The ideas in this paragraph reflect conversations with Mary Kelly, February 1992.

17. Deutsche, "Alternative Space," p.62.

18. Neil Smith, "Tompkins Square Park Timeline," in *Krzysztof Wodiczko. New York City Tableaux: Tompkins Square, The Homeless Vehicle Project* (New York: 1989), p.15.

19. Rosalyn Deutsche and Cara Gendel Ryan, "The Fine Art of Gentrification," *October*, no.31 (Winter 1984), p.93.

20. Smith, "Tompkins Square Park Timeline," pp.16-17.

21. Ibid.

22. Ibid., p.17.

23. Deutsche, "Alternative Space," p.60.

24. Quoted in Julie Courtney, "The Homeless Vehicle Project: Philadelphia," in *Krzysztof Wodiczko. New York City Tableaux*, p.41.

25. Smith, "Tompkins Square Park Timeline," p.20: "December 22-24: As temperatures remained well below freezing, four homeless people freeze to death in the city this weekend."

26. Raymond Williams, "Base and Superstructure in Marxist Cultural Theory," in *Problems in Materialism and Culture: Selected Essays* (London: Verso, 1969), p.37.

WORKS IN THE EXHIBITION

*Dimensions are in inches; height precedes width precedes depth. An asterisk (*) indicates that the work is being presented in the form of photographic documentation only.*

VITO ACCONCI
(b. 1940)
Following Piece, 1969
(recreated 1992)
Black-and-white photographs with printed text mounted on board, 30 x 40
Collection of the artist; courtesy Barbara Gladstone Gallery, New York

0 to 9, Street Works, No. 6, Supplement, 1969
Mimeographed booklet, 11 x 8 1/2
Collection of Jean-Noël Herlin

DENNIS ADAMS
(b. 1948)
Bus Shelter II, maquette, 1984
Aluminum, plexiglass, wood, enamel, Duratrans, and fluorescent light on wood base, 15 3/4 x 23 1/2 x 17 1/2
Collection of the artist; courtesy Kent Fine Arts, New York

Bus Shelter IV, maquette, 1987
Aluminum, plexiglass, wood, enamel, Duratrans, and fluorescent light on wood base, 22 1/8 x 33 5/8 x 26 1/4
Collection of the artist; courtesy Kent Fine Arts, New York

Bus Shelter VIII, maquette, 1988
Aluminum, plastic, Duratrans, and fluorescent light on wood base, 14 1/4 x 32 x 23 1/2
Collection of the artist; courtesy Kent Fine Arts, New York

La Pissotière, maquette, 1988
Plexiglass, enamel, Duratrans, and fluorescent light on wood base, 17 1/2 x 33 1/4 x 12 1/4
Collection of the artist; courtesy Kent Fine Arts, New York

MICHAEL BANICKI
(b. 1956)
Storefront Rating, 1991
1000 black-and-white photographs, 5 3/8 x 6 each; paper legend, 44 1/2 x 10 1/2; pine box, 7 x 66 x 7 /12
Collection of the artist; courtesy Feature, NewYork

JEAN-MICHEL BASQUIAT
(1960-1988)
The Bond, Earle or Stanhope, 1982
Oil paintstick on canvas, 45 3/4 x 40
Estate of the artist; courtesy Robert Miller Gallery, New York

JEAN-MICHEL BASQUIAT
AL DIAZ
* Frames from *New York Beat*, 1981
Directed by Edo Bertoglio
Courtesy Maripol

STANLEY BROUWN
(b. 1935)
This Way Brouwn, 25-2-61, 26-2-61, 1961
Book, 9 5/16 x 7 7/8
Collection of Jean-Noël Herlin

1 Step—100,000 Steps, 1972
Book, 10 5/8 x 8 1/16
Collection of Jean-Noël Herlin

DANIEL BUREN
(b. 1938)
Seven Ballets in Manhattan, 1975
Offset poster, 17 1/16 x 22
Jean-Noël Herlin Archive, New York

* *Seven Ballets in Manhattan*, May 27-June 2, 1975
Photograph courtesy John Weber Gallery, New York

Legend I and *Legend II*, 1972
2 books, 13 x 20 each
Private collection

ANDRÉ CADERE
(1934-1978)
Galerie des locataires, 1973
Offset paper, 11 5/8 x 8 3/16
Jean-Noël Herlin Archive, New York

Histoire d'un travail, 1982
Book, 11 5/8 x 8 5/16
Collection of Jean-Noël Herlin

SOPHIE CALLE
(b. 1953)
The Shadow, 1985
10 black-and-white pho-
tographs and 12 printed
texts, 80 x 130 overall
The Bohen Foundation,
New York

HENRY CHALFANT
(b. 1940)
Composite photograph of
Trap/Dez/Daze, 1979-83
Photograph by the artist

GUY DEBORD
(b. 1931)
*Guide psychogéographique de
Paris,* 1957
Map, 23 5/8 x 29 1/8
Collection of Thomas Y.
Levin

ÖYVIND FAHLSTRÖM
(1928-1976)
✴ *Bob Hope Mao Tse Tung
Demonstration from "Kisses
Sweeter than Wine",* 1966
Experiments in Art and
Technology Archive,
Berkeley Heights,
New Jersey

✴ *Bob Hope Mao Tse Tung
Demonstration from "Kisses
Sweeter than Wine,"* 1966
Experiments in Art and
Technology Archive,
Berkeley Heights,
New Jersey

THÉODORE FRAENKEL
(1896-1964)
*Excursions DADA: Saint
Julien le Pauvre,* 1921
Graphite on paper,
8 1/8 x 5 3/16
The Gilbert and Lila Silver-
man Fluxus Collection

*Excursions & Visites DADA:
1ère Visite: Église Saint Julien
le Pauvre,* 1921
Letterpress, 10 7/8 x 8 5/8
The Gilbert and Lila Silverman Fluxus Collection

GRAFFITI ARTISTS
6 piece books, c. 1982-91,
by SPIDER, KIES,
RAMELLZEE, JOEY, TDS
CREW, LADY PINK
Mixed media, dimensions vary
Collection of Martin Wong

ILONA GRANET
(b. 1948)
Curb Your Animal Instinct,
1986
Silkscreen on metal,
24 x 26
P.P.O.W, New York

No Cat Calls, 1987
Silkscreen on metal, 24 x 24
P.P.O.W, New York

HANS HAACKE
(b. 1936)
*Shapolsky et al. Manhattan
Real Estate Holdings, a Real-
Time Social System, as of
May 1, 1971,* 1971
2 maps, 24 x 20 each; 6
charts, 24 x 20 each; text
panel, 24 x 20; 142 black-
and-white photographs, 10
x 8 each; 142 typewritten
pages, 10 x 8 each
Collection of the artist

DAVID HAMMONS
(b. 1943)
✴ *Cold Shoulders,* 1990
Installation at Jack Tilton
Gallery, New York

✴ *Bliz-aard Ball Sale,*
Cooper Square, Exit Art,
New York, 1983

KEITH HARING
(1958-1990)
✴ Photograph of *Crack Is
Wack,* 1986
Estate of Keith Haring

JENNY HOLZER
(b. 1950)
✴ Selections from *Truisms,*
Times Square, New York,
1982;
Barbara Gladstone
Gallery, New York

TEHCHING HSIEH
(b. 1950)
One Year Performance,
1981-82
4 offset posters, 17 x 11 each
Printed text, 11 x 8 1/2
Collection of Jean-Noël
Herlin

DOUGLAS HUEBLER
(b. 1924)
*New York-Boston Exchange
Shape,* 1968
2 panels, 24 x 28 each:
2 maps and typewritten
page, 11 x 14 each; 4 black-
and-white photographs,
8 x 10 each
Collection of the artist;
courtesy Holly Solomon
Gallery, New York

*Variable Piece #1, New York
City,* 1968
5 panels, 24 x 28 each: map
and typewritten page, 11 x
14 each; 12 black-and-white
photographs, 8 x 10 each,
on 4 panels
Collection of the artist;
courtesy Holly Solomon
Gallery, New York

Duration Piece #10, 1969
2 mimeographed typewritten pages, 11 x 8 1/2 each
Jean-Noël Herlin Archive, New York

Alternative Piece, Paris, 1970, 1970
2 panels, 24 x 28 each; 6 black-and-white photographs, 3 x 5 each; typewritten page, 14 x 11; map, 14 x 11 Collection of the artist; courtesy Holly Solomon Gallery, New York

Variable Works (in Progress) Düsseldorf, Germany-Turin, Italy, 1970-71
Offset paper, 14 x 8 1/2
Jean-Noël Herlin Archive, New York

Internationale Situationniste, no.1 (June 1958)
Collection of Peter Wollen

CANDY JERNIGAN
(1951-1991)
Found Dope, 1986
Assemblage on paper, 22 1/2 x 30
Collection of Philip Glass

Found Dope II, 1986
Assemblage on paper, 27 x 39
Collection of Philip Glass

ALLAN KAPROW (b. 1927)
MARTA MINUJIN (b. 1944)
WOLF VOSTELL (b. 1932)
A Three Country Happening (New York, Berlin, Buenos Aires), 1966, Offset lithograph, 17 3/4 x 16 7/8
The Gilbert and Lila Silverman Fluxus Collection

ON KAWARA
(21,697 days on May 19, 1992)
I Got Up, September 4, 5, 11, 17, 22, 1968. 5 postcards, 3 3/8 x 5 5/16 each
Collection of John Evans

I Got Up, December 20, 21, 22, 23, 24, 25, 1970
6 postcards, 4 x 5 3/4 each
Private collection

I Went, September 4, 5, 11, 17, 22, 1968; December 20, 21, 22, 23, 24, 25, 1970
11 photocopied maps with ink, 11 x 8 each
Collection of the artist

BARBARA KRUGER
(b. 1945)
✱ *Untitled (Questions)*, 1991
Mary Boone Gallery, New York

GEORGE MACIUNAS
(1931-1978) et al.
Free Flux-Tours, May 1976
Offset poster, 12 3/16 x 9
The Gilbert and Lila Silverman Fluxus Collection

LOIS NESBITT
(b. 1959)
Gallery Labels, 1992
Plexiglass plaque, 3 x 6; 49 stick-on labels, 3 x 6 each; photocopied maps, 8 1/2 x 11
Collection of the artist

CLAES OLDENBURG
(b. 1929)
Proposed Monument for the Intersection of Canal Street and Broadway, New York: Block of Concrete Inscribed with Names of War Heroes, 1965
Crayon and watercolor on paper, 20 x 16
Collection of Alicia Legg

YOKO ONO
(b. 1933)
Scores:
"City Piece," winter 1961
"Map Piece," summer 1962
"Wind Piece," fall 1962
"City Piece," fall 1963
"Map Piece," spring 1964
Printed sheets, 5 x 5 each
Courtesy of the artist

ALAIN PAIEMENT
(b.1960)
Building Site 1992
(half-scale version), 1992
Color photographs on 6 laminated panels, 69 x 69 x 69
Collection of the artist

BENJAMIN PATTERSON
(b. 1934)
Invitation-map for Benjamin Patterson's Exhibit at Robert Filliou's Galerie Légitime, Followed by a Fluxus Sneak Preview, 1962
Offset lithograph, ink, and marker, 7 7/8 x 18 3/8
Collection of Jon Hendricks

REPOHISTORY
The Lower Manhattan Street Sign Project, 1992
Silkscreen on metal, 24 x 18; printed text, 10 x 8 1/2; photocopied maps, 9 1/2 x 6 1/2
Collection of REPOhistory, New York

ALDO ROSSI
(b. 1931)
South Bronx Academy of Art (model), 1991
Wood, brass, paper, paint, 7 1/4 x 20 1/2 x 20 1/2
Aldo Rossi/Studio di Architettura, New York

Il Centro Culturale e Scolastica nel Bronx, 1991
Ink and watercolor on paper, 23 x 25
Aldo Rossi/Studio di Architettura, New York

Site Plan for the Academy, 1991
Ink and watercolor on paper, 17 x 20
Aldo Rossi/Studio di Architettura, New York

Perspective Sketch, 1991
Ink and watercolor on paper, 17 x 20
Aldo Rossi/Studio di Architettura, New York

North Elevation, 1991
Blueprint, 18 x 22
Aldo Rossi/Studio di Architettura, New York

Longitudinal Section, 1991
Blueprint, 18 x 22
Aldo Rossi/Studio di Architettura, New York

Site Plan, 1991
Blueprint, 18 x 22
Aldo Rossi/Studio di Architettura, New York

South Elevation, 1991
Blueprint, 18 x 22
Aldo Rossi/Studio di Architettura, New York

EDWARD RUSCHA
(b. 1937)
Every Building on the Sunset Strip, 1966
Book, 7 1/16 x 5 1/2
Private collection

GARY SIMMONS
(b. 1964)
Everlast Champion, 1991
Mixed media, 35 x 14 x 5
Collection of Linda Glass and Jeffrey Mercer; courtesy Roy Boyd Gallery, Chicago

FRANCESC TORRES
(b. 1948)
Assyrian Paradigm, 1980
(recreated 1992)
Playing cards, electric motor, aluminum, and plexiglass, dimensions variable
Collection of the artist

ANDY WARHOL
(1925-1987)
Birmingham Race Riot, 1964
Silkscreen on paper, 20 x 24
The Andy Warhol Foundation for the Visual Arts, Inc.

DAN WILEY
(b. 1962)
The Two Waterfronts, 1989
4 black-and-white photographs, 39 1/2 x 29 1/2 each; 1 black-line blueprint, 60 x 44
Collection of the artist

KRZYSZTOF WODICZKO
(b. 1943)
The Homeless Vehicle, 1989
Welded aluminum, nylon cloth, and mixed media, 54 x 27 x 57
Collection of the artist; courtesy Exit Art, New York

DAVID WOJNAROWICZ
(b. 1954)
Arthur Rimbaud in New York, 1978-79
Black-and-white photograph, 8 x 10
P.P.O.W, New York

Arthur Rimbaud in New York, 1978-79
Black-and-white photograph, 8 x 10
P.P.O.W, New York

Arthur Rimbaud in New York, 1978-79
Black-and-white photograph, 8 x 10
P.P.O.W, New York

Arthur Rimbaud in New York, 1978-79
Black-and-white photograph, 8 x 10
The New York Public Library, Astor, Lenox, and Tilden Foundations; Photography Collection, The Miriam and Ira D. Wallach Division of Art, Prints, and Photographs

Arthur Rimbaud in New York, 1978-79
Black-and-white photograph, 8 x 10
The New York Public Library, Astor, Lenox, and Tilden Foundations; Photography Collection, The Miriam and Ira D. Wallach Division of Art, Prints, and Photographs

Arthur Rimbaud in New York, 1978-79
Black-and-white photographs, 8 x 10
The New York Public Library, Astor, Lenox, and Tilden Foundations;Photography Collection, The Miriam and Ira D. Wallach Division of Art, Prints, and Photographs

VIDEOTAPES

TONY COKES
(b. 1956)
Black Celebration, 1988
Videotape, black-and-white,
sound, 17 minutes
Distributed by Drift
Distribution, New York

TEHCHING HSIEH
(b. 1950)
One Year Performance,
1981-82
Directed by Robert
Attanasio, Videotape transfer
from film; color, sound,
60 minutes
Collection of Gilbert and
Lila Silverman

MATT MULLICAN
(b. 1951)
Untitled, 1991
Videotape, color,
30 minutes
Courtesy Ministère de la
Culture et de la Communi-
cation, Paris, and Michael
Klein Inc., New York

YOKO ONO
(b. 1933)
JOHN LENNON
(1948-1980)
Rape, 1969
Videotape transfer from film;
color, sound, 77 minutes
Collection of Yoko Ono

FRANCESC TORRES
(b. 1948)
*Belchite-South Bronx: A
Trans-Historical, Trans-Cultur-
al Landscape*, 1987-88
Videotape, color and
black-and-white, sound,
39 minutes
Distributed by Zoom
Television, Barcelona

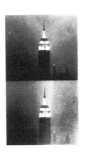